AN INTRODUCTION TO MUTUAL FUNDS WORLDWIDE

....

Ray Russell

BICENTENNIAL
1807
WILEY
2007
BICENTENNIAL

John Wiley & Sons, Ltd

Other Wiley Editorial Offices

John Wiley & Sons Inc., 111 River Street, Hoboken, NJ 07030, USA

Jossey-Bass, 989 Market Street, San Francisco, CA 94103-1741, USA

Wiley-VCH Verlag GmbH, Boschstr. 12, D-69469 Weinheim, Germany

John Wiley & Sons Australia Ltd, 42 McDougall Street, Milton, Queensland 4064, Australia

John Wiley & Sons (Asia) Pte Ltd, 2 Clementi Loop #02-01, Jin Xing Distripark,
Singapore 129809

John Wiley & Sons Canada Ltd, 6045 Freemont Blvd, Mississauga, ONT, L5R 4J3, Canada

Wiley also publishes its books in a variety of electronic formats. Some content that appears in
print may not be available in electronic books.

British Library Cataloguing in Publication Data

A catalogue record for this book is available from the British Library

ISBN 978-0-470-06203-6 (PB)

Typeset in 12/16pt Trump Mediaeval by SNP Best-set Typesetter Ltd, Hong Kong
Printed and bound in Great Britain by TJ International Ltd, Padstow, Cornwall, UK
This book is printed on acid-free paper responsibly manufactured from sustainable forestry in
which at least two trees are planted for each one used for paper production.

CONTENTS

PREFACE

....

This introductory guide seeks to reflect the growth and importance across the globe of mutual funds as a means of investing in worldwide economic development, whether to build a fund for retirement or otherwise.

My aim has been to provide the reader with a basic appreciation of mutual funds in their many forms, in the hope that, apart from proving a useful reference, it will stimulate further exploration of the subject and encourage still greater appreciation, advocacy and use of the mutual fund as a sensible, efficient and ultimately rewarding means of investment, suitable for the vast majority of people.

The guide covers the origins, purpose, development, uses, operation and regulation of mutual funds and, where appropriate, draws attention to similarities and differences between major jurisdictions, commenting on their unique features and approaches, if any.

I am indebted to the industry's trade bodies, statistical firms and regulatory authorities for placing so much helpful material on their web-sites, sources that I heartily commend to any serious student or potential investor.

Neither the publishers nor I accept any responsibility for actions, claims or losses arising out of the use of information contained in this guide.

Ray Russell
London, October 2006

ABOUT THE AUTHOR

Ray Russell FCMA, FCIS, MSI, CertPFS, ACOI is the Principal of GCR Management Services, a consultancy and training organisation he founded in 1988 to provide informed, personalised and practical advisory and training services to investment businesses and professional bodies.

His experience includes 20+ years in senior positions with prominent British and American investment banks and 10 years as a director of a UK fund management and administration group of companies. He has served on the Investment Management Association's (IMA, formerly AUTIF) Executive, Regulations, Audit and Training Committees and is chair of its Collective Investment Schemes Technical Discussion Group and of the Securities & Investment Institute's Qualifications Assessment Board for its Investment Administration Qualification (IAQ).

Chapter

1

....

INTRODUCTION

The objective of this guide is to explain what *mutual funds* are, how they have developed and how they are used, regulated and administered across the globe. Both open-ended and closed-ended funds are described and, where appropriate, the differences between the international markets, particularly USA, Europe and UK are addressed.

We tend to use the word 'funds' to mean both the hard cash that constitutes the initial capital that is available for investment and also for the 'vehicle' or medium through which the resulting investments are made and managed.

Thus, 'personal funds' comprise the cash in our pockets and the balances in our bank accounts, some of which can be thought of as 'committed funds', needed to cover current expenditure, and some of which may not be required for some time, but nonetheless is earmarked for a future event. If there's any surplus beyond these two types of commitment, apart from being among the fortunate few, we have 'spare funds'.

What we choose to do with our spare funds – and, indeed, with the funds that are not required until some time in the future – is a personal matter. We may regard spare funds as 'fun money' and opt to spend them on whatever takes our fancy. We shall hopefully take a responsible attitude to funds set aside or building up to meet future commitments or ambitions, but nevertheless may feel we can afford to place at least some of these funds, as well as 'spare' funds, into an 'investment', rather than leaving them to the potential ravages of inflation, whether as uninvested cash or as interest-earning 'savings'. The problem and the challenge is knowing how to select investments that meet our objectives for return and suit our appetite for risk.

This is where the second use of the word 'funds' comes in.

1.1 COLLECTIVE INVESTMENT

Most individuals lack substantial wealth or enough wealth to make the investment of their personal funds directly into stocks and shares a practical and low-risk endeavour. Equally, most people lack the professional expertise and knowledge of economics, business, markets and individual companies to identify the sheep from the goats, or the wheat from the chaff as it were. Then, of course, there's the time and paperwork associated with keeping track of a personal portfolio, and with keeping an eye on taxation opportunities and obligations, especially tricky if it's a global portfolio.

Mutual funds offer a solution. They are a form of *collective investment*. They allow any number of investors to pool their individual investments and thereby participate in a larger and more diversified portfolio of investments than would otherwise be possible. The advantages and commercial benefits of pooling the often modest savings or spare money of a large number of individuals have long been manifest in the form of collective schemes managed centrally by organisations that can provide all the necessary investment and administrative services. The participants in a mutual fund can take advantage of specialised professional management and reduced administration and, depending on the relevant tax regime, obtain some taxation benefits.

In its simplest sense, the 'mutual fund' could be run informally from the local club or pub, possibly as an investment club, but, for the purposes of this guide, we are talking about broader-based offerings from institutions such as banks, life companies, asset managers, stockbrokers and specialist investment houses – institutions that themselves use mutual funds as an efficient way of marshalling and managing their clients' assets as well as the investments they set aside to support their main business, e.g. as life assurers or pension providers.

Collective investment schemes or even more generically *'pooled funds'* or *'investment funds'* may be found worldwide, with varying structures and with a variety of names. For example:

- USA – mutual funds, closed-end funds, unit investment trusts;
- Canada – mutual funds;
- EU – Undertakings for Collective Investment in Transferable Securities (UCITS);
- France and Luxembourg – Société d'Investissement à Capital Fixe (SICAF) or Organismes de Placement Collectif en Valeurs Mobilières (OPCVMS) which can be either:

- ○ Société d'Investissement à Capital Variable (SICAV) or
  - ○ Fond Commun de Placement (FCP);
- Italy – SICAV, Cos'è Fondo Comune di Investimento;
- UK – investment trusts, unit trusts, open-ended investment companies (OEICs or ICVCs – investment companies with variable capital) and, for charities, common investment funds;
- South Africa – unit trusts;
- Australia – investment trusts, insurance bonds, superannuation funds;
- Hong Kong – unit trusts, mutual funds (investment companies);
- Japan – investment trusts, investment companies;
- China – bond funds, investment funds.

Individual mutual funds may be further classified according to their:

- **asset orientation**, e.g. as stock or equity funds, bond funds, securities funds, money funds, futures and options funds, property or real estate funds or mixed or hybrid funds;
- **investment objective**, e.g. growth funds, income funds, balanced funds and, for funds that seek to emulate the performance of an index, index or tracker funds.

'Hedge funds' constitute a further variation. Although they may properly be classified as 'growth funds', they are unlike other funds, which are typically 'long-only' funds. Hedge funds deploy a variety of strategies, including short-selling and derivative positioning across

a range of asset classes, in an attempt to make profits in both a rising and a falling market. Consequently, they are sometimes referred to as *'absolute return funds'*.

Still further differentiations can be found in fund structures, e.g.:

- where one fund invests exclusively in one other (master fund and feeder fund); or in a number of other funds (fund of funds);
- has itself a number of sub-funds (umbrella fund).

Yet another distinction between funds arises due to their legal structure. Funds may be constituted as companies, as trusts or as partnerships or they may have a joint ownership structure but no legal personality (such as the French FCP). Finally, a comparatively recent development, since its introduction in Canada in 1989, is the exchange traded fund, a fund which tracks an index but is bought and sold as a listed company.

1.2 HISTORY

Switzerland can lay claim to the earliest mutual fund – 'Société Civile Genèvoise d'Emploi de Fonds' was established in 1849 – although when the UK's Foreign & Colonial Company set up its 'Foreign and Colonial Government Trust' in 1868, it could claim to have been the first to define the term 'investment funds':

Vehicles which provide the investor of moderate means with the same advantage as large capitalists in diminishing risk in foreign and colonial stock by spreading the investment over a number of stocks.

With some refinements, this definition holds good today and Foreign & Colonial can rightly claim to have founded, if not the mutual funds industry, certainly the investment trust industry, due to the way it responded to a threat – arising around the turn of the 19th century – of a legal challenge to the effectiveness of a trust structure for the purpose of holding investments. Instead of confronting the challenge, F&C converted its stable of 'investment trusts' to investment companies, whilst keeping the name 'investment trust' for those companies, which, of course, ceased to be trusts. A number of its emulators and imitators followed suit but a number did not and, to this day, the trust structure remains popular in the UK and elsewhere in the world, though not in mainland Europe.

Other developments around this time included the first mutual fund to be set up in the USA – the 'Boston Personal Property Trust', established in 1894 – and the first in Germany – the 'Zickertische Kapitalverein', in 1923.

All these early funds originally took the form of a 'fixed trust', in which each unit represented a proportion of a fixed investment portfolio. These trusts were also what we term today 'closed-ended', i.e. funds with a fixed number of units or shares in existence that could not be increased or reduced. Typically, neither the investments nor the participants could be varied during the fixed life or duration of the trust. Only on arrival of the previously fixed termination date and the winding-up of the trust could investors realise their investment, assuming the portfolio still had some value!

The disadvantages of such a structure must quickly have become apparent and if the fledgling mutual fund industry were to survive, a more flexible, open-ended arrangement was needed. Open-ended or flexible funds are the antithesis of the original fixed trusts: investors may come and go as they please, the investment portfolio may be varied at any time and the fund does not have to have a fixed life.

Mutual funds as open-ended funds were first formed in the USA, again starting in Boston, in 1924, with 'The Massachusetts Investment Trust', but the start of the growth of mutual funds in the US awaited the introduction of the Investment Company Act of 1940. In the UK, it was 1934 before the first truly flexible fund was launched – 'The Foreign Government Bond Trust'.

In continental Western Europe, investment funds have been in existence only since the 1940s and, in the former communist bloc of Eastern Europe, development was delayed until comparatively recently, typified by closed-end voucher privatisation funds. Pan-European development followed the adoption by EU Member States of the first UCITS Directive, which, in 1985, gave us another definition of 'investment funds':

Vehicles the sole objective of which is the collective investment in transferable securities of capital raised from the public and which operates on the principle of risk spreading.

This UCITS Directive was designed to allow funds established and authorised in one Member State to be marketed across borders into the other countries making up the EU and the European Economic Area without further authorisation. Luxembourg and Dublin capitalised on this development and quickly became leading administrative centres for the establishment of funds to be marketed across Europe.

Elsewhere, although mutual funds are present in China, India, South Africa and South America and many other countries, their prominence outside the USA and the larger European countries is confined to Canada and Australasia. Significant recent growth has been registered in Hong Kong and Australia, the latter now boasting more funds and more funds under management than Japan despite the latter's record and reputation for saving and having established nearly 3,000 funds since its fresh start in 1951.

Although the Swiss got there first, the mutual fund as we know it today was essentially a British invention, refined firstly by Americans and then by Europeans and exported across the globe. Mutual funds are now the single most important investment vehicle for an ever-growing world population, particularly as a means of providing a source of income and wealth for life after retirement from employment.

According to statistics published by the American Investment Company Institute ('ICI') in its Factbook 2006, the total worldwide assets invested in mutual funds at the end of 2005 was a staggering $17.8 trillion, with well over half this figure – $9.5 trillion – invested in US registered investment companies and trusts, and with nearly 50% of US households owning mutual funds. These figures exclude the estimated further trillion dollars invested in hedge funds.

1.3 CONSTRUCTION AND AUTHORISATION

Construction

Mutual funds are constructed either as *investment companies* or as *trusts*. The difference between the two forms is significant as it affects ownership of the underlying assets and the nature of participants' interests in those assets. In some jurisdictions, they are known, respectively, as the *corporate type* and the *contractual type*. Either form may be open-ended or closed-ended, but the term 'mutual fund' is usually reserved for the open-ended form.

- In the *company* form, participants (shareholders) own shares in the company and the company owns the underlying assets; shareholders have no direct or indirect rights or interest in those assets, only rights in and arising from their ownership of shares in the company.
- In the *trust* or *contractual* form, the legal owner of the underlying assets is the trustee; the participants or members of the scheme are the beneficiaries under

the trust and, therefore, the *beneficial owners* of the underlying assets.

- Closed-ended funds are usually constructed as investment companies and listed on the local stock exchange. It is also possible, although unusual, Dublin and Luxembourg apart, for open-ended funds to be exchange-listed.

In practice, regulations ensure that each form follows similar requirements and gives similar rights and protections to participants, whether share- or unit holders. As a result, the legal differences have little bearing on day-to-day operation, although in the case of an umbrella fund established as a company, were a deficiency of assets to arise in one sub-fund, it must be transferred to and therefore be borne by the other sub-funds.

Like many jurisdictions, the US allows both constructions, referring to its most common form of mutual fund as a *management company* and the other form as a *business trust*. The US also has what is known as a unit investment trust, which is both unmanaged and closed-ended.

In the UK, the investment trust is also closed-ended and a company. Open-ended investment is available through:

- Unit trusts – a trust form;
- Open-Ended Investment Companies (OEICs) known to the UK regulators as investment companies with variable capital (ICVCs) – a company form.

Elsewhere in the EU, the form is usually a company modelled on the French SICAV – Société d'Investissement à Capital Variable – an open-ended investment company. In Asia and the Far East, both forms exist and, like the US, sometimes side-by-side, as in Hong Kong and China. Until 1998, Japan only allowed the open-ended trust form.

Authorisation

Authorisation is usually a matter for an agency of the Finance Ministry of the country concerned and, depending on the country's regulatory structure, may distinguish between authorisation to conduct business as a management company and authorisation to market a particular fund. Typically, a mutual fund cannot be established for marketing to the general public without first being *authorised* for that purpose by the designated central authority of its home country or province.

Such authorisation may carry rights or potential rights to market in other countries as well. For example, a fund set up anywhere in the European Union and meeting the requirements of the EU's directive for UCITS is theoretically freely marketable in the other EU countries. Invariably, however, a further registration or recognition process is necessary to satisfy the host nation that its marketing rules will be observed. Selected countries' authorising and regulatory bodies, as outlined earlier, are summarised below:

Country	Senior authority	Responsible authority
USA	Federal Reserve Board	SEC – Securities and Exchange Commission
UK	HM Treasury	FSA – Financial Services Authority
Canada	Ministry of Finance	Provincial Securities Commissions Canadian Securities Administrators
China	Ministry of Finance	People's Bank of China CSRC – China Securities and Regulatory Commission
France	Ministry of the Economy and Finance	AMF – Autorite des Marches Financiers
Germany	Federal Ministry of Finance	BAFin – Federal Financial Supervisory Authority
Hong Kong	Legislative Council of Government	SFC – Securities and Futures Commission MPFA – Mandatory Provident Fund Schemes Authority

Country	Senior authority	Responsible authority
India	Government of India	SEBI – Securities and Exchange Board of India
Ireland	Minister for Finance	IFSRA – Irish Financial Services Regulatory Authority
Italy	Ministry for the Economy & Finance	Banca d'Italia CONSOB – Commission Nazionale per la Società e la Borsa
Japan	Ministry of Finance	FSA – Financial Services Agency
Korea (Rep)	Ministry of Finance and Economy	FSC – Financial Supervisory Commission
Luxembourg	Institut Monétaire Luxembourgeois	CSSF – Commission de Surveillance du Secteur Financier

1.4 GROWTH AND DEVELOPMENT
Growth

Growth of the industry worldwide has been sporadic, with significantly accelerated growth in more recent years. Development in the major markets over the 30 years to the end of 2005 is demonstrated by the value of their publicly offered funds' aggregate net asset values as at 31 December for the years shown:

	USA	UK	France	Japan
1975	$50bn	£1,4bn	N/A	¥2,470bn
1985	$430bn	£20,3bn	FF643bn	¥19,972bn
1995	$3,028bn	£112.5bn	FF2,665bn	¥47,999bn
2000	$7,248bn	£261.1bn	Euros 766.1bn	¥49,399bn
2005	$9,518bn	£317.8bn	Euros 1,155bn	¥55,348bn
2005 in US$	$9,518bn	$547bn	$1,363bn	$470bn

(Detailed statistics as at 31 December 2005 are shown on pages 23 & 24.)

Measures of genuine growth are difficult to pin down or attribute. The industry typically measures itself by reference to 'funds under management (FUM)' or 'net asset value (NAV)' but these are amalgams of the effects of incoming and outgoing investors, falls and rises in the stock-market value of the funds' portfolios, the creation of new funds and the winding-up of others, not to mention the difficulties inherent in comparing across the world's various currencies. Comprehensive statistics covering all these aspects are simply not available, so we are left to accept the industry's preferred measure and to express data in either local currency or the US$. Individual countries do publish data on the value of sales (i.e. new money) and of the number of accounts on fund registers (which are indicators of popularity) but these data are not available as readily as FUM or NAV.

Development

Whilst there have been scares and scandals, growth has been steady and sometimes spectacular, with funds under management worldwide now approaching US$18 trillion. In America alone, mutual funds are held today by an estimated 91 million individual investors, with nearly US$9 trillion in mutual fund shares and another US$½ trillion in other registered investment companies and trusts. This is well over 50% of the worldwide total, an estimated 20% of the total US savings market, and a penetration of over 50 million US domestic households.

The tables on pages 23 and 24 chart the year-end statistics for the world's mutual funds, in terms of numbers of funds and value of net assets. The substantial growth evident during the 1990s can be explained by a number of reasons:

- An increasing number of investors began to appreciate the advantages of investing through mutual funds.

- Fund managers were inventive about the types of fund and related facilities on offer.
- Governments and corporations encouraged and assisted growth via retirement plans based upon mutual funds.
- Regulators gradually introduced more permissive regimes in terms of the controls and limitations on funds that may be offered to the general public.
- Strong performance of bull markets worldwide.

Come the dawn of the new millennium, and bear market conditions gripped most of the world and lasted into 2003, since when a steady recovery has occurred. During that bear market, the aggregate value of funds under management in mutual funds fell commensurate with the falls in stock markets worldwide from a peak at the end of 2000 of almost $12 trillion to a little over $10.5 trillion at the end of September 2002, 75% of which can be attributed to the USA. Other individual countries showed both positive and negative movements in US$ terms during this period but, of those showing a higher NAV at the end of 2002, only France, Ireland and Luxembourg of the major markets could boast continued year-on-year growth – most were below a peak reached in the first half of 2002. The comparisons are complicated by the weakness of the US dollar during the period, which boosted the decline, as many countries experienced much lower asset decreases measured in local currencies.

Generally, there was some recovery in the fourth quarter of 2002 but a worldwide total of some US$11.3 trillion remained below the level at the end of 1999. For some countries, the fall was from a peak achieved around that time; Spain, for example, peaked at the end of 1998, taking 5 years to the end of 2003 to recover. Italy, the UK, Japan, New Zealand and the Republic of Korea, all peaked at the end of 1999 and while most recovered by the end of 2003, Korea's recovery came at the end of 2004 and Japan has yet to fully recover. In the US, the fall came later (2001 to 2002) and the recovery quicker (2002 to 2003).

Notwithstanding the fall in NAV experienced by individual mutual funds during 2000–2002, their popularity as an investment medium continued to grow and the rate of growth is still accelerating.

The Canadian experience is typical: it took 60 years for the Canadian mutual fund industry's value of funds under management to reach C$100 billion. It took 4½ years to reach the next hundred billion, only 18 months to reach the third hundred billion and little more than a year to break through C$400 billion (US$280 billion), in 2000. There was a falling off in 2001 and 2002, but recovery since then has been a remarkable 80% to US$490 billion at the end of 2005. Perhaps more remarkable is the more than ten-fold increase in the seven years from 1990 to 1997, from C$25 billion to C$285 billion. Although now comfortably above its 2000 NAV peak, the number of funds available for investment, which grew from just over 1,600 at the end of 2000 to over 1,900 in 2002, has now fallen back to just under 1,700.

Brazil is the other significant contributor to the Americas total, with almost 1,000 more funds than Canada (2,685) and over US$300 billion at year-end 2005, slightly more than double its level at the end of 2000.

In Asia, and particularly in Australia and Hong Kong, after earlier highs and lows, in terms of new money coming into funds and disregarding the effect on NAV of the crash of 1987 and the 2000–2002 bear market, steady growth has been experienced since the 1980s.

Hong Kong saw growth in 1999 alone of 85% in local currency terms and a near-doubling from 1998 to 2000 to more than HK$1,500 billion (US$196 billion). Interestingly, Hong Kong is one of the few places where growth (in local currency terms) was restored in 2002 to levels reached in 2000 after dipping during 2001 to below its 2000 peak. Although total NAV fell back by the end of 2002, by the end of 2005 it had tripled to US$460 billion and growth in the number of funds has continued unabated – from around 700 in 1997 to over 1,000 in 2005.

Elsewhere in Asia, Australia now boasts the highest NAV at US$700 billion, significantly ahead of Hong Kong, which is now slightly behind a recovering Japan, who saw 40% growth in 2005 to reach US$470 billion.

The European experience has varied from country to country and, in aggregate, exceeded 50% of the NAV of funds registered in the USA in 2002 (now 67%), even though Europe has consistently offered between three and four times the USA's number of funds. In fact, the number of funds available in the USA has remained fairly steady, at between 7,300 and 8,300 but falling over the last four years to under 8,000, while Europe's offerings have grown from 20,000 to 30,000. Significantly, Europe experienced a more than 10% higher level of net sales than the USA in 2005.

Meaningful comparisons are readily made between the countries of the European Union (EU) since 1999 when all of the major players but the UK adopted the euro as a common currency. France and Luxembourg jockey for first position, together accounting for almost 50% of the European total, and Ireland, Italy and the UK a further 25%. All five have experienced significant growth in the number of funds (see table on p. 23) but the NAV picture tells another story. All but Italy experienced growth in 2000 and both Italy and France have dipped below subsequent peaks in 2004 by the end of 2005, to leave Luxembourg the clear number one with net assets of Euros 1,387 billion (US$1,635 billion) ahead of France's Euros 1,155 billion (US$1,363 billion).

Alone on the African continent as regards registered mutual funds, South Africa has experienced a staggering near four-fold increase in NAV from 2000, growing from US$16.9 billion to US$65.6 billion at end-2005.

The first quarter of 2006 has seen the growth continue. Worldwide there were over 58,000 funds with more than US$19 trillion in assets under management at 31 March, with all regions experiencing just over or just under 10% increases over the end-2005 values.

Future developments

Future developments are likely to take the form of a wider and more varied application of the product, rather than structural development of the product itself. There may be refinements and added features, but the core product that has evolved is a sound model for collective investment.

Regulators are beginning to relax the constraints on the nature of assets that may be held in a mutual fund accessible by the public and we may see more 'mixed funds' and 'hedge funds' being offered. In this vein, the EU has recently updated its UCITS Directive ('UCITS III') and this significantly broadens the scope for mixed funds and derivatives funds, as well as increasing the permitted level of investment in a single asset.

The 'mutual fund company' is now the most common universal form but the legal forms of mutual fund that exist worldwide may be subject to change and greater harmony. The UK, for instance, only comparatively recently introduced an open-ended investment company structure – to allow its products to be better understood outside the UK, particularly in mainland Europe, than its traditional unit trust.

A further recent development that has more distance to travel, so to speak, is the way in which charges are levied and management performance rewarded. As investors become more aware and knowledgeable about investment, and the need for active selling diminishes, they will trend toward 'no-load' funds, funds that do not levy initial, sales or preliminary charges on entry or exit charges on redemption, but rely upon annual management fees.

Pressure is also beginning to grow from investors and managers alike for 'performance-related' fees. The usual basis of remuneration is a fixed percentage of net asset value at prescribed points in time, with no specific allowance or adjustment for good or poor performance. In most countries, remuneration for retail fund managers based on performance is either not allowed or is restricted to particular types of fund – the hedge fund is one such. However, a growing sophistication on the part of investors could lead to broader application of an approach that gives the manager a larger fee when performance has exceeded benchmark than when it doesn't – 'why should poor performance be rewarded?' is a question that will be asked more frequently.

Impetus for growth can also be expected from industry efforts to improve and extend access via electronic exchanges and to present the advantages of the product to an ever-increasing number of people requiring a home for pension contributions or like savings.

Recent statistics

The following table displays the growth in number of funds and, for most countries/regions, the decline and revival of NAV over the last 5 years. Figures are as at 31 December (* = *not available*) and exclude hedge funds and funds of funds; totals may not agree due to rounding and/or the absence of individual country figures. China is a notable absentee.

	Number of funds			Net assets (US$ million)		
	2000	2002	2005	2000	2002	2005
AMERICAS	**12,549**	**13,884**	**13,763**	**7,419,549**	**6,776,289**	**9,763,919**
Argentina	226	211	200	7,425	1,021	3,626
Brazil	2,097	2,755	2,685	148,538	96,729	302,927
Canada	1,627	1,956	1,695	279,511	248,979	490,518
Chile	*	226	683	*	6,705	13,969
Costa Rica	122	128	110	919	1,738	804
Mexico	305	364	416	18,488	30,759	47,253
United States	8,172	8,244	7,974	6,964,667	6,390,358	8,904,822
EUROPE	**25,524**	**28,972**	**30,053**	**3,296,015**	**3,463,000**	**6,002,249**
Austria	760	808	881	56,549	66,877	109,002
Belgium	918	1,141	1,391	70,313	74,983	115,314
Czech Republic	70	76	51	1,990	3,297	5,331
Denmark	394	485	471	32,485	40,153	75,199
Finland	241	312	333	12,698	16,516	45,415
France	7,144	7,773	7,758	721,973	845,147	1,362,671
Germany	987	1,092	1,076	238,029	209,168	296,787
Greece	265	260	247	29,154	26,621	32,011
Hungary	86	90	91	1,953	3,992	6,068
Ireland	1,344	1,905	2,127	137,024	250,116	546,242
Italy	967	1,073	1,035	424,014	378,259	450,514
Liechtenstein	*	111	200	*	3,847	13,970
Luxembourg	6,084	6,874	7,222	747,117	803,869	1,635,785
Netherlands	494	680	515	93,580	84,211	94,357
Norway	380	419	419	16,228	15,471	40,122
Poland	77	107	150	1,546	5,468	17,652
Portugal	195	170	169	16,588	19,969	28,801
Romania	16	20	23	8	27	109
Russia	37	57	257	177	372	2,417
Slovakia	*	*	43	*	*	3,035
Spain	2,422	2,466	2,672	172,438	179,133	316,864
Sweden	509	512	464	78,085	57,992	119,059
Switzerland	368	512	510	83,059	82,622	116,669
Turkey	*	242	268	*	6,002	21,749
UK	1,766	1,787	1,680	361,008	288,887	547,103

	Number of funds			Net assets (US$ million)		
	2000	2002	2005	2000	2002	2005
ASIA/PACIFIC	**13,167**	**10,794**	**12,668**	**1,134,302**	**1,063,857**	**1,939,251**
Australia	*	*	*	341,955	356,304	700,068
Hong Kong	976	942	1,009	195,924	164,322	460,517
India	243	312	445	13,831	20,364	40,546
Japan	2,793	2,718	2,640	431,996	303,191	470,044
Korea (Rep)	8,242	5,873	7,279	110,613	149,544	198,994
New Zealand	629	577	563	7,802	7,505	10,332
Philippines	18	21	32	108	474	1,449
Taiwan	156	351	459	32,074	62,153	57,301
S. AFRICA	**149**	**460**	**617**	**16,291**	**20,983**	**65,594**
WORLD	**51,574**	**54,110**	**56,863**	**11,866,788**	**11,324,129**	**17,771,366**

Sources: European Fund and Asset Management Association (EFAMA); Investment Company Institute (ICI), USA.

Chapter

2

....

THE MANAGEMENT
OF FUNDS

2.1 WHO RUNS MUTUAL FUNDS?

Mutual funds are run by professional *fund managers*, who may choose to appoint other professional bodies to undertake, under contract, one or more aspects of running their funds, such as:

- investment managers – to manage the portfolio of investments;
- marketing companies – to advertise and promote the funds;
- selling agents – to actively sell the funds' shares or units;
- administrators – to perform accounting and servicing functions;
- registrars or transfer agents – to maintain the registers of share- or unit holders.

Sometimes, it is the trustee of a trust who not only has responsibility for the safe custody of fund assets but also has responsibility for maintenance of the register of holders. More typically it is the manager who fulfils that duty, if necessary by delegated appointment by the trustee. Regulations typically require that the manager does not perform the function of custodian of fund assets, and that this is the responsibility of an independent *custodian*, *depositary* or *trustee*, in whose name the fund's assets are to be held or registered.

Though these third parties are usually regulated firms themselves and appointed by the manager, they are accountable to the shareholders and the regulators for the safe-keeping of the fund's assets, whether under their control directly or via the services of a sub-custodian. This is one function that may not normally be delegated to the manager, any more than the manager may delegate the function of investment management to the custodian, depositary or trustee. This separation of responsibility is at the heart of investor protection, although, of course, protection is limited to safe-keeping and does nothing to protect against falling markets or incompetent portfolio management.

Another usual regulatory requirement is for the manager's obligations to maintain records and to prepare accounts to be subject to audit by a qualified person or firm, typically a 'registered auditor'. The frequency of an audit may vary but auditors are usually required to examine the books and records at least once a year and to report to the fund's shareholders annually.

Compliance with detailed regulations governing the operation and marketing of a fund is the direct responsibility of the manager but the auditor and, in certain key respects, such as valuation, pricing and investment constraints or limits, the custodian/ depositary/trustee will have duties of oversight.

A number of factors and considerations determine the extent to which a manager will 'outsource' functions, including restrictions imposed by regulations. Much will depend upon the background of the management firm and why it has become involved with investment funds. Managing its clients' investments, particularly its smaller clients' portfolios, through the medium of a mutual fund, is a natural, economic and administratively convenient step for a stockbroker or asset manager to take and it is likely that it will perform all the necessary functions itself. By contrast, a firm that has established a mutual fund on the back of its reputation in a non-investment field will almost certainly rely on specialist third parties to provide it with all the necessary functionality. Examples from the UK include Marks & Spencer and Virgin, together with several of the banks and building societies that set up investment funds as a defensive measure to avoid the loss of deposit funds when investment returns are superior. As a general matter, outsourcing administrative functions, particularly registration/transfer agency and fund accounting but also dealing and investor servicing, has seen significant growth in recent years.

2.2 WHAT'S IN A NAME?

The names managers give to their mutual funds will typically convey some idea of investment objective and possibly of investment policy, but rarely indicate whether the fund is a trust or a company. Most jurisdictions have an accepted acronym or designation for companies established under their laws, such as 'Inc.', 'plc', 'Ltd', but these are rarely used, or required to be used, by unlisted investment funds structured as companies and there is no designation to identify that a fund is structured as a trust.

Open-ended and closed-ended funds

Whether a fund is open- or closed-ended is another feature not conveyed by the fund's name, although the designation 'ICVC' is used as a suffix to the fund's name by some UK OEIC managers, to denote a fund that is, in regulatory language, an 'Investment Company with Variable Capital' but this practice is not mandatory or widespread.

Open-ended funds are ones that are authorised to have a *variable amount of capital* in issue. Shares or units are issued to investors whenever they pay in a lump sum or make subscriptions by way of a regular savings scheme. Unless the manager has a stock of shares available from a prior creation of new shares or from departing investors, he must arrange for the fund to receive payment for a further creation of new shares. When investors want to leave the fund, they sell their shares or units back to the fund manager, who is said to redeem or repurchase such shares. The manager may cancel any shares redeemed or he may elect to reissue them to an incoming investor.

Closed-ended funds have a predetermined, *finite amount of capital* in issue. New shares or units cannot be created or cancelled on a day-to-day basis. Investors wishing to buy or sell shares or units must do so by transacting with other investors, typically through a stock exchange. Regulators usually insist upon a stock exchange listing for closed-ended funds that are to be publicly marketed, such as investment trusts in the UK. Closed-ended mutual funds often have a fixed duration, typically 10 or 20 years. Most open-ended funds have no fixed end date.

2.3 BENEFITS OF MUTUAL FUNDS

Institutions obtain administrative and, sometimes, taxation benefits by using mutual funds to manage their own assets. Such funds are invariably not available to the general public. Funds that are authorised to be promoted to the general public (frequently referred to as *'retail funds'*), usually extol the *benefits* to the private individual, namely:

Small investment required

Although both minimum holdings and minimum initial amounts are usually required, individuals can invest comparatively small sums of money in mutual funds, particularly through plans that accept regular subscriptions. So-called 'small investors' can thereby obtain the benefits of worldwide economic activity (hopefully growth) rather than allowing these to be enjoyed by the banks (and their shareholders) and others with whom they deposit their funds in return for an interest income.

Spread of risk

By 'risk' we typically mean the risk that our investment will depreciate in value or, in the extreme, cease to

have any value. In the context of a portfolio of investments, there are two aspects to risk and therefore to
risk-spreading. The first is the effect that failure of any
one share within the portfolio has on the value of the
whole portfolio; the second is the effect of general news
or events on the prices of all shares, either across the
market or on particular sectors of the market. These two
aspects each have their own response when constructing
a portfolio – the number of holdings and their spread
across geographic regions, industry and economic sectors
and asset types:

(a) **Number of holdings:** Money supplied by the
participants is invested in a number of different
securities in order to reduce the risk of loss associated
with any one investment, known to fund managers
as 'unsystematic' or idiosynchratic' risk, as distinct
from the risk that the whole market may fall, known
as 'systematic' or 'market' risk. A typical fund invests
in 50–100 companies in an attempt to eliminate
unsystematic risk. If a participant invested his money
directly into the shares of one company, he could
lose all of it if the company went into liquidation.
Within a mutual fund's broadly based portfolio, only
a relatively small amount would be lost as a result
of the failure of a single investment.

(b) **Geographic, industry or economic sector and asset
type spread:** This is referred to as *diversification*.
While nearly all funds offer a spread, not all offer
diversification and all but the 'balanced' or 'hybrid'
fund offer only limited diversification. A truly
diversified portfolio is one that has investments in

several different regions, industries, sectors, and asset types, thereby reducing systematic risk inherent in any one market.

While a large number of holdings will reduce, even eliminate, unsystematic risk, the remaining systematic risk will be large if the holdings are concentrated in the same region or sector. While gains or superior performance may sometimes be achieved by having all one's eggs in the same basket, if the basket falls out of favour, it doesn't matter that it was holding a large number of eggs. Investors in specialist funds, whether industry or country specific, such as technology or Japan funds, can attest to significant losses in recent years, even though their investments were in funds with portfolios of over 100 individual stocks, because the industry or economic sector failed to live up to expectations. It is also the case that diversified but equity-only funds will tend to fail investors in years when there are widespread falls across the major markets, whereas bond funds generally maintain the value of their holdings. While this might suggest that cautious investors should be steered towards international or global balanced funds for the substantial part of their portfolios, even here, currency risk remains a threat to wealth!

Professional fund management

Very few individuals have sufficient time or expertise to manage their own wealth with the same degree of competence as a professional. The money invested in a mutual fund is managed by professional fund managers, who have access to a wide range of resources and research data and are 'close to the market', able to spot trends and opportunities as they arise. Unlike the individual investors in the fund, who have other matters on their mind, the professional fund manager can concentrate on achieving the investment objectives of the fund.

Cheaper dealing

Although the individual participant's investment can be small, pooling the contributions of many investors into a single fund allows the investment manager to deal in large quantities and therefore at a lower cost than the individual investor could achieve. While this differential is being eroded by the increasing use of internet dealing, it remains significant and is most marked when the manager has responsibility for a number of funds and utilises a central dealing desk to aggregate or 'bulk' portfolio managers' orders for execution in the market.

Convenience

A single holding in a mutual fund can be equivalent to a portfolio of possibly 100 individual investments but without the attendant difficulties of monitoring their individual performance and periodically adjusting the composition of the portfolio. Buying and selling shares or units in a mutual fund is easy, and may be effected directly with the manager without the need for an intermediary. In some circumstances it can be accomplished by telephone and, increasingly, via the Internet or a dedicated electronic exchange. In most countries, the prices of mutual funds' shares or units are required to be published in national newspapers, so it is a simple matter on any day to determine the value of the particular mutual fund investment – certainly more convenient than performing 100 different calculations!

Reinvestment of income

Many mutual fund managers offer schemes that enable income to be automatically reinvested, either by purchasing additional shares or units, usually without the imposition of an initial charge, or by the use of an alternative share or unit type – the 'accumulation' share. This facility is particularly useful if the investor wishes to build a holding and does not need income. Whenever circumstances and hence requirements change, it is normally a simple matter to change to and from automatic reinvestment by advising the manager.

Taxation

Deferral of (but not exemption from) tax is a common benefit. In some countries, mutual funds enjoy tax benefits that are incorporated in the construction of the product. For example, in the UK, unit trusts and OEICs are exempt from capital gains tax (CGT) when the manager sells fund investments at a profit. This enables the value of the fund to grow faster than would be the case if tax were to be extracted on realisation of a gain.

Any tax attributable to gains is collected from the individual investors upon realisation of a gain on their mutual fund holding.

2.4 USES OF MUTUAL FUNDS

Mutual funds are used by private investors and by institutions for different but overlapping reasons:

Private investors use mutual funds to invest money in the hope that it will:

- grow in value, or
- provide income, or
- deliver both, i.e. capital growth and income

either to serve specific financial needs, now or in the future, or simply to enhance their prospect of wealth.

Institutions, particularly life companies and pensions funds, use mutual funds as a convenient way to organise and manage some if not all of their investment portfolios, which will have objectives similar to those of the private investors who are the ultimate beneficiaries.

Asset managers may use mutual funds as a means of managing the portfolios of their smaller clients, when segregated or discrete management is inappropriate, unnecessary or not required.

Intermediaries or advisory firms may well recommend mutual funds to their clients, particularly if sums to be invested are comparatively modest and insufficient to achieve the desired diversification or spread of risk.

Ways of investing

The two most common ways of investing directly in retail mutual funds are:

- lump sum ('one-off' payment)
- regular contribution or subscription (usually monthly, with an automatic transfer of money from a bank account). This can also be achieved by reinvesting periodic income generated by the underlying holding.

Investing may also be *indirect*. For example, part of the premium for a life policy might be invested in one or more mutual funds, as might contributions to a pension plan.

Direct investment usually requires completion of an application form and payment in advance.

Cost averaging

An investor regularly investing a fixed sum of money, buys more shares or units when prices are low, and fewer when prices are high. The effect is to achieve an average price paid that is lower than the average price over the same period. For example:

Month	Price	Investment	Shares/Units
1	0.25	50.00	200
2	0.50	50.00	100
3	1.00	50.00	50
TOTAL		150.00	350

Average cost per share/unit purchased:
   (150.00/350) = 0.43
Average share/unit price:
   (0.25 + 0.50 + 1.00 divided by 3) = 0.58

Investing regularly also smooths out the effect of falls and rises in prices over the period of investment. By comparison with investing the same amount in a lump sum at the beginning of the period, the regular contributor gains greater value when the price recovers.

Month	Price	Investment	Shares/Units
1	1.00	50.00	50
2	0.50	50.00	100
3	0.25	50.00	200
4	1.00	50.00	50
Total		200.00	400
Value at Month 4		400.00	

Lump sum of 200.00 invested in Month 1 bought 200 shares/units. Value at Month 4 is 200.00 compared with 400.00 for the same amount invested in four regular instalments of 50.00.

Of course, if the price is continually rising, as in the first table, then the investor buying in a lump sum at the beginning of the period is better off than the regular contributor by the end of the period. More typically, prices are volatile when, without assured timing skills, investing regular contributions (and thereby averaging) is favoured.

Safe but not risk-free

In most countries, the regulations stipulate an important safeguard, whereby a fund's individual holdings are to be registered in the name of an independent custodian or trustee, to ensure that investment in mutual funds is safe, in the sense that the assets cannot be misappropriated by the manager or by the investment adviser. However, this does not prevent fund prices fluctuating, reflecting the value of the underlying investments, and therefore, although ownership is secure, the value of an investment in mutual funds can fall as well as rise.

As with any investment portfolio, a mutual fund can be used for all or any of the following:

Overseas investment

Research material and dealing facilities may be difficult to access outside an investor's domestic market, so some investors, who may nonetheless be prepared to select direct investments in companies based in their own country, use mutual funds to provide exposure to overseas economies.

Investing for children

Parents and particularly grandparents are often moved to settle sums of money on their offspring, whether for a particular purpose or simply to fulfil a wish to 'give them a start in life'. Mutual funds are a perfect 'home' for such sums and the grandparents, for example, can set up an investment account for their grandchildren. The holdings can subsequently be transferred to the children's own names when they reach a suitable age, 18, 21 or 25.

Retirement income

Governments around the world are increasingly admonishing their citizens to make provision for their old age; many offering tax incentives by way of special plans or accounts. As with any known or specific future liability or commitment, mutual funds are again perfect vehicles for accumulating retirement funds. Investors can build up a holding in a mutual fund while in employment via savings from salary to achieve a holding that can provide income and a capital 'cushion' against the financial requirements of old age. Depending on tax legislation, the investor may or may not have freedom of access to funds held in retirement or pension plans and decisions have to be made about how much is to be invested in such plans and how much in other 'unfettered' funds.

Mortgage repayment

Repayment of a loan to purchase a house is a common future commitment. Many lenders acknowledge that mutual funds are a sensible vehicle for accumulating the sum required to repay a mortgage debt, particularly if held in a tax-efficient plan and may even operate funds themselves for the purpose of accepting regular contributions. It is essential to monitor the value of the investment regularly to ensure that it is growing as expected, and to make adjustments to the regular investment amount if necessary.

2.5 RANGE OF INVESTMENT AIMS

The statistics presented earlier illustrate just how large is the number of mutual funds available. Each fund has specific investment objectives and investment policies, which determine the nature and level of risk; the greater the risk, the greater should be the potential reward. The range of funds available provides a wide spectrum, from very safe, low-risk funds investing in government securities to speculative, high-risk funds investing in new or smaller companies or emerging markets or being highly geared or utilising sophisticated techniques involving derivatives.

Each investor needs to determine his or her *risk profile* – the nature and level of risk or uncertainty about future returns that he or she is prepared to accept in relation to the intended use of the mutual fund investment. Only then can an appropriate fund be selected. Some investors may have different risk profiles for different segments of their portfolio, according to purpose, and all investors have a changing profile as they near retirement:

- for mortgage repayment a low-risk investment would be sensible, but, if the term is long enough, greater risk could be taken in the early years;
- similarly for pension or retirement provision; greater risk can be taken when the investor is young;
- if saving to provide a 'start in life' for children, low-to-medium risk funds should perhaps be chosen;
- if investing a windfall, such as a legacy, a relatively high risk might be acceptable, on the basis that the funds arose unexpectedly, although hopefully without being reckless.

Some mutual funds are designed to respond to particular risk requirements or appetites by holding *specialised* or *'exotic'* investments. These could include:

- companies operating in emerging markets – countries whose financial services industries are at an early stage of development;
- companies dealing in commodities, such as gold or oil;
- property, either directly or via holdings in property companies;
- derivatives, such as futures and options.

2.6 PERFORMANCE STATISTICS

Investors should routinely review the performance of their investment in a mutual fund; there are, however, some factors that need to be considered and understood, as regards both the preparation and the use of statistics.

The most readily available performance statistics are compiled to generate a 'league table' based upon the value of an investment after given time periods since the date of initially investing a particular sum of money, say £1,000.

The numbers are calculated assuming the initial investment is made at the buying, or offer, price and the number of shares thus acquired are valued at the current selling, or bid, price. To avoid distortions caused by different patterns of income, the numbers are adjusted on the assumption that any income entitlement is reinvested at each date during the period when the fund made an income distribution. This overall approach is cited as being on the basis of 'offer to bid, income reinvested'.

In addition to presenting a comprehensive listing, publishers usually group the funds for which they have calculated performance into the categories or sectors specified by the trade association. Care must be exercised when using the resultant tables to evaluate the performance of particular funds by individual investors.

Comparisons are valid only between similar products and for the same period. Comparing the performance over one month of a property fund with the five-year performance of a Japanese equities fund would not provide any meaningful information. Nor is it especially instructive to compare a bond fund with an equity fund, unless one is considering a switch. Similarly, the tables assume that, aside from the reinvestment of income, no other investment is made during the period, whether lump sum or via a regular savings plan. The tables are of limited use therefore to the investor who builds up a holding by making regular contributions.

The important considerations are:

The category or type of the fund – most mutual fund trade associations define performance categories, which are used in magazines that publish statistics. The fund's investment objectives and/or its chosen asset class will determine which category is appropriate.

The timescale of comparison – typical timescales are one, three and six months, and one, five and ten years. Some managers look only for long-term performance and ignore the short term, and investors need to watch their investments with this in mind.

Which attributes are being compared – attributes include:

- capital growth;
- net income;
- gross income;
- capital growth, including reinvested (net or gross) income;
- total return.

Inflation – inflation tends to make investment performance look good, especially in graphical form. While it is possible to reduce the apparent effect of inflation by using scaling techniques, investors are better advised to assess *real returns* – the return after deducting the rate of inflation. Alternatively, or additionally, an index, such as a retail prices index that shows the effect of inflation, can be included in the graph.

Volatility – the calculations present performance between two specific dates but not the extent to which performance has varied during the period defined by those dates. Some agencies now supply a measure of volatility, usually in terms of *standard deviation*, or will present a simple rating of 'high', 'medium' or 'low'.

Manipulation – statistical techniques can be applied to the data to provide unrepresentative, distorted or misleading information. Advertising standards, if in place, will inhibit the use of any such misrepresentation but investors need to be aware that statistics can be used to prove just about anything.

Chapter

3

....

REGULATION

T his chapter covers the background and purpose of regulations, describes how a mutual fund is created and presents the regulations affecting fund management, marketing and administration, and those designed to protect investors.

3.1 BACKGROUND AND PURPOSE

The primary purpose of *regulations* is to protect investors, and the roots of governmental regulation of mutual funds in the longer-established markets are often associated with major scandals and market crashes.

In the USA, the stock market crash of 1929 prompted an extensive investigation by Congress into the securities industry. It revealed that overselling, or 'ramping' of shares, particularly radio company shares, had created unrealistic expectations and false, overvalued markets. The investigation resulted finally in the *Investment Company Act 1940*, which established the Securities and Exchange Commission (SEC) – this Act remains the cornerstone of US mutual fund regulation – and the *Investment Advisers Act 1940*. Along with two Acts passed into Federal law in the 1930s – the *Securities Act 1933* and the *Securities Exchange Act 1934* – these four Acts provide the bulk of federal powers over the activities of US investment companies. In fact, the only addition to US legislation affecting all companies since 1940 is the Sarbanes-Oxley Act of 2002 and that has only an indirect bearing on mutual funds themselves, being more concerned with accounting, auditing and disclosure practices of trading companies, following the Enron and Worldcom scandals.

The Investment Company Act requires all funds to register with the SEC and to meet certain operating standards; the Securities Act mandates specific disclosures; the Securities Exchange Act sets out anti-fraud rules covering the purchase and sale of fund shares; and the Investment Advisers Act regulates fund advisers. The SEC is charged with overseeing the mutual fund industry's compliance with all these regulations, although the funds themselves are organised under State laws – as corporations or business trusts.

The depression of 1929 also affected Europe and the UK, where the London Stock Exchange recommended the regulation of fixed trusts in 1935. A Board of Trade report the following year concluded that, whilst unit trusts met an investment need, some form of legislation was necessary to protect the public. Formal regulation took a little time to implement and the *Prevention of Fraud (Investments) Bill 1939* did not become law until August 1944. This Act was replaced in 1958 and whilst various committees and advisers published recommendations for further reform, little was changed until the *Financial Services Act 1986*, which repealed all earlier legislation.

As in all European countries that are members of the European Union, UK legislation in 1986 had to take account of the European 'UCITS Directive' of 1985 (*UCITS: Undertakings for Collective Investment in*

Transferable Securities). This itself had been the long-anticipated effort to unify investment regulation across the Member States of the European Union, following the widespread fraud perpetrated by Bernie Cornfeld's Investors Overseas Service organisation, involving 'pyramid selling' of funds from a base in Switzerland. The UCITS Directive has been the subject of recent amendments and Member States are at varying stages of implementing national legislation to harmonise regulation of funds across the EU.

Having experienced 10 years of so-called 'self-regulation' under the Financial Services Act, major changes to the regulatory structure in the UK were announced in 1997. The Securities and Investments Board (SIB) subsequently was renamed the Financial Services Authority (FSA) and eventually absorbed the separate regulatory powers and responsibilities of the self-regulatory organisations (SROs) established under the 1986 Act, as well as the supervisory responsibilities of the Bank of England, the authorisation and prudential supervision responsibilities of the Department of Trade and Industry in relation to insurance companies and of the registrars of Building and Friendly Societies, and those of the UK Listing Authority in place of the London Stock Exchange.

By the time the Financial Services and Markets Act 2000 became effective at midnight on 30 November 2001, the FSA was responsible for the regulation and supervision of all companies operating in the UK, whose main business is banking, insurance or investment, and of their senior management and other key employees.

A significant number of firms, such as lawyers and accountants, who conduct investment business but only as an ancillary to their main activities continue to be regulated by their respective professional bodies. By contrast, the FSA has recently taken on responsibility for direct regulation of insurance and mortgage advisers.

This creation of a single regulator (except for pensions, for which there is a separate Pensions Regulator) brings the UK, in relation to investment business, much closer to the USA model, where the Securities and Exchange Commission has been the sole regulator since 1940. In making the FSA responsible for virtually all financial businesses, the UK has taken the model a stage further than the USA, where banks are still regulated by the Federal Reserve Board and State Banking Commissions.

Elsewhere, regulation has typically followed or been taken from US or UK models, depending upon which country has had the most influence in post-war developments, but influenced by local experience, good and bad, of initial legislation. A summary level description of the current law and regulatory structure of a number of these countries follows:

Australia – the first unit trust to be offered in Australia was named just that – Hugh Dalton's Australian Fixed Trusts offering units in the First Australian Unit Trust in late 1936, when the funds industry was largely unregulated. The Australian retail funds market is now fully regulated under the provisions of the *Managed Investments Act* (MIA) and, more recently, the Financial Services Reform Act of 2001, which changed the licensing and disclosure requirements. The MIA requires managers to take on the duties and obligations of the *single responsible entity*, whereby they are obligated under statute law to uphold unitholder rights. Under this arrangement, trustee duties have been fused with manager duties, but whilst external custody is not mandatory, the majority of managers use independent custodian services. Superannuation funds also gain the regulatory protection of the MIA, as approximately 90% of these savings are invested in wholesale and retail MIA vehicles. Another development has been Financial Sector Reform legislation – after six years of planning and development, the Financial Sector Reform package commenced on 11 March 2002. Under this regime, financial institutions are subject to harmonised disclosure and reporting obligations. Licensing of dealers and advisers in securities has been strengthened, as has the requirements for training of individuals who give consumers financial advice. The new arrangements entail substantial and far reaching changes in fund management companies and other financial institutions, and are being phased in over a two-year period. Supervision is the responsibility of the Australian Financial Services Commission. The Investment and Financial Services Association plays a significant part in imposing standards and guidelines on its 100 members, who account for some A$900 billion invested by 9 million households, over 95% of the total.

Canada – laws and regulations are made and enforced by each province and territory, which has its own securities regulator, a government agency usually known as a 'Securities Commission'. Representatives from each commission serve on an umbrella body, the Canadian Securities Administrators, which occasionally creates national rules. In addition, the Mutual Fund Dealers Association of Canada (MFDA) and the Investment Dealers Association of Canada (IDA) have been formed as Self Regulatory Organisations (SROs) to regulate specific industry groups within certain provinces. SROs are not government agencies but member bodies that operate subject to the oversight of the Securities Commissions.

China – although funds have existed in China since 1991, the initial experience was unsatisfactory and, in November 1997, the *Provisional Regulation on the Management of Securities Investment Funds* was published. The new regulation led to the launch of Jintai Fund and Tianyuan Fund on 23 March 1998, marking a new beginning for China's fund management industry. Current legislation became effective on 1 July 1999 – the *Securities Law of the People's Republic of China* – but as elsewhere, this is to be upgraded by a new piece of legislation, the *Investment Fund Law*. Regulatory responsibilities were shared between the People's Bank of China and the China Securities Regulatory Commission, but the latter is now responsible for the detailed regulation of funds and fund management companies. An important role is also played by the *Securities Association of China*, established in 1991 but reformed in 1999 under the current legislation to exercise self-regulation over its members. SAC revised and improved its charter for this purpose in 2002.

France – the most important piece of legislation governing French mutual funds is its Law of 23 December 1988, an Act governing collective investment schemes, actually enacted by decree in September 1989. It replaced two 1979 Acts, which governed SICAV and FCP structures separately, with a single set of regulations, and implemented the 1985 UCITS Directive. Detailed regulations are set out in Application Decrees and Orders dated December 1998 and any points concerning SICAVs not covered in these laws are governed by general legislation, in particular the basic company law dated 24 July 1966. The 1993 Investment Services Directive was implemented by the 1996 *Financial Activities Modernisation Act* which governs fund management companies, who are also subject to regulations issued by the supervisory authority, originally 'COB' – *Commission des Opérations de Bourse*, which merged following the Financial Securities Act 2003 with CMF *Conseil de marches financier (Consultative Council of Asset Management)* and CDGF *Conseil de discipline de la gestion financiere (Disciplinary Council of Asset Management)* to form the new regulator AMF *Autorite des Marches Financier* – whose approval is required before fund units or shares can be offered to the public. AMF is also responsible for routine monitoring of fund management companies' compliance with rules governing portfolio composition, reports to investors and marketing materials. And now also for what was an element of self-regulation that prevailed through the active participation of industry professionals in the two merged Councils. CDGF investigated breaches of codes of conduct or other infractions of the rules and could impose warnings, fines or suspensions for breaches of professional ethics and violations of any statutes and regulations that apply to investment funds. The ultimate authority is the Ministry of the Economy and Finance.

Germany – a new law, the Financial Markets Promotion Act, which came into force on 1 July 2002, modernised German investment law. Among other things it is now possible to have different share classes for one fund and open-ended real estate funds are allowed to invest worldwide as long as currency risks are limited to 30% of net assets. Also, from 1 May 2002, under amendments to the 1994 Securities Trading Act, the previously separate supervisory offices for banking, insurance and investment were brought together into a new single regulator – BAFin – Federal Financial Supervisory Authority, responsible to the Federal Ministry of Finance for all aspects of supervision. BAFin has three aims stipulated under the law – investor protection, market transparency and market integrity – and pursues these through the issue of regulations, ordinances and guidelines.

Hong Kong – the *Securities and Futures Ordinance* enacted in March 2002 and operational from April 2003, combined into a single ordinance all previously existing ordinances for the regulation of the securities and futures markets, principally the 1974 *Protection of Investors Ordinance* and the *Securities Ordinance*. Hong Kong also has a series of Codes, the first of which – the *Code on Unit Trusts* – was enacted in 1978, when the *Committee on Unit Trusts* was formed to administer the Code. Under the Securities Ordinance, the Securities and Futures Commission (SFC) became the statutory body charged with protecting investors in Hong Kong's securities and futures markets and is responsible for authorising funds, for regulating intermediaries engaged in dealing or advising, including licensing, and for regulating the marketing of funds to the investing public. The SFC is assisted in its regulatory functions by the Committee on Unit Trusts, which comprises industry professionals among others and acts as an advisory body; the *Investment-Linked Assurance Committee* and *Pooled Retirement Funds Committee* for other types of funds were formed in 1991 when new Codes were enacted for each of the three fund types.

India – the mutual fund industry started in India in 1964 with the formation of the Unit Trust of India, registered under a separate Act of Parliament. Other public sector institutions entered the business in 1987 but it was not until 1993 that the first of the private sector participants commenced operations. Regulatory responsibility resides with the Securities and Exchange Board of India ('SEBI'), which published its Mutual Fund Regulations in 1996 and amended them in January 2006 to widen the permitted investment powers to include gold and goldrelated instruments. Although not a self-regulatory organisation, the trade body, AMFI (Association of Mutual Funds in India) works closely with SEBI in the development of rules and regulations and is influential

in the area of conduct of business, publishing its Code
of Ethics in 1997, which has all the hallmarks of
regulatory principles, and introducing its certification of
intermediaries programme in July 2000. SEBI has made
AMFI certification compulsory for advisers.

Ireland – development of a mutual fund industry dates
effectively from the establishment of the IFSC – the
International Financial Services Centre – under legislation
passed in the late 1980s as one of a number of
measures to stimulate growth and employment in an
otherwise poorly performing economy and capitalising
on the EU's UCITS Directive. The significant majority
of funds established in Ireland are open-ended investment
companies, usually listed on the Dublin Stock Exchange,
designed for marketing throughout Europe. Under the
Irish *UCITS Regulations 1989*, the Central Bank of
Ireland was made responsible for authorising and
supervising investment and insurance intermediaries
but the *Central Bank and Financial Services Authority
of Ireland Act 2003* established on 1 May 2003 a single
regulatory framework for the financial services industry
and created the Irish Financial Services Regulatory
Authority (IFSRA), with its own board and chief executive
reporting directly to the Minister for Finance. Other
relevant legislation includes the *Unit Trust Act 1990*,
the *Companies Acts 1963 to 1999*, the *Investment
Limited Partnership Act 1994* and the *Investment
Intermediaries Act 1995*.

Italy – primary regulatory responsibility lies with the
central bank – Banca d'Italia – under the *Banking Law* or,

more formally, *Legislative Decree 385 of 1 September 1993*, and *Law 410 of 23 November 2001* in relation to real estate funds. Essentially, the Bank of Italy authorises banks that provide investment services and other companies that engage in collective asset management. Investment firms are authorised by the separate public authority responsible for regulating Italy's securities markets, CONSOB – *Commission Nazionale per la Società e la Borsa*. CONSOB operates under Legislative Decree 58 of 24 February 1998, amended in 2005 and which introduced consolidated law on financial intermediation and was implemented by regulation on 1 July 1998. CONSOB has subsequently passed a series of detailed regulations and resolutions in common with other European regulatory authorities on matters such as capital adequacy, money laundering and market abuse.

Japan – funds analogous to investment trusts existed in Japan in 1937 in the form of investors' associations, which, like the UK's Foreign & Colonial Company's original investment trust, faced challenges of legality and were dissolved in 1940, to be replaced in 1941 by undertakings that, modelled on the UK's unit trust, found legal support. Post-war confusion led to these funds becoming closed to new investment in August 1945 and final dissolution in February 1950. Patterned on the USA's Investment Company Act of 1940, Japan's *Securities Investment Trust Law* was passed in June 1951, providing the legal basis for the type of investment trusts now in operation. Originally, these investment trusts were established to meet the changing requirements of government policy to popularise securities investment, thereby providing much-needed capital for the rehabilitation and reconstruction of business operations and production facilities, rather than in response to economic growth and investor demand, as elsewhere in the world. The responsible body at that time was the Securities and Exchange Commission but this body was abolished in 1952 and its functions taken over by the Ministry of Finance, which retained responsibility for the authorisation and regulation of investment businesses and funds until June 1998, when responsibility transferred to the Financial Supervisory Agency, which in turn gave way to the Financial Services Agency in July 2000. The MoF introduced amendments to the law in 1967 and *Guidelines for Licensing Investment Trust Management Companies* in 1989, revising them in 1992. Continuing depression of Japan's stock market from 1990 brought about deregulatory reforms, firstly in late 1994/early 1995, then a package of measures in 1997 and finally reform of the law, effective in December 1998, to make Japan's system comparable with those in operation in the USA and Europe. Still further amendment occurred in 2000, when the law was renamed the *Law for Investment Trusts and Investment Companies.* This law allows for funds established as securities investment trusts (known as *contractual type funds*) to have broader investment objectives/policies than previously (e.g. to invest in real estate), and to be either publicly offered or privately placed trusts, and also makes provision for funds to be established as investment companies (known as *corporate type funds*). In June 2006 the Financial Services Agency proposed a new legislative framework for investor protection, the *Financial Instruments and Exchange Law*, containing far-reaching reforms and consolidation of existing laws to bring Japan into line with the rest of the developed world's approach to financial services.

Korea – like Japan, Korea in the late 1960s needed to mobilise domestic capital to facilitate long-term, stable financing of large-scale industrial and infrastructure projects. The securities investment industry naturally attracted special attention and the *Securities Investment Trust Business Act (SITBA)* was passed in 1969, to allow the setting up of contractual-type investment trusts, and the first of these, *Korea Investment Corporation*, was launched that year. Under SITBA, which was implemented by related Presidential Decrees and Enforcement Ordinances, the Ministry of Finance and Economy had, by 1989, authorised three investment trust companies to undertake operations nationwide and five in provincial areas to distribute investment trusts in Seoul and in their respective specified regional areas. Gradual reform of the financial markets began in the mid-1990s and restrictions on the establishment of new investment trust companies were lifted in 1996, only for the currency crisis of late 1997 to reverse the growth that had been achieved. Corporate-type investment funds, labelled *SICs – Securities Investment Companies* – and referred to as mutual funds, were introduced in late 1998 under the SICA – Securities Investment Companies Act. Earlier that year, responsibility for the approval and supervision of financial companies passed from the Ministry of Finance and Economy to the newly-established Financial Supervisory Commission and its enforcement arm, the

Financial Supervisory Service. Matters of policy and the making or amending of laws and regulations remained with the Ministry. Both SITBA and SICA were upgraded by amendments in April 2002 and implemented by Enforcement Decrees on 26 September that year. Significant among the changes that were introduced was the role of KITCA – *Korean Investment Trust Companies Association.* KITCA had been established under the SITBA in 1996 to represent the management companies but, since the amendment, is now the responsible body for formulating and revising the standard trust deed and is the body that managers must notify when they set up funds within the scope of the standard deed. SITBA, SICA and the investment advisory part of the *Securities Exchange Act* were replaced in August 2003 by AMBA – the *Indirect Investment Asset Management Business Act,* a comprehensive law based on SITBA to combine the previous legislation.

Luxembourg – the authority responsible for supervision and control of the financial sector in Luxembourg is the IML – Institut Monétaire Luxembourgeois – a creation of the 1983 laws to regulate Undertakings for Collective Investment, which first appeared in 1959. The subsequent *Law of 30 March 1988* rendered Luxembourg the first EU Member State to incorporate the 1985 UCITS Directive into national legislation and positioned it to take advantage of the cross-border marketing opportunities available to complying funds. The law has been updated by IML Circular of 29 January 1991 and extended by further legislation – *Law of 19 July 1991* – relating to UCIs for institutional investors and the *Law of 8 June*

1999 concerning pension funds. The 1988 law permits funds to be set up as either common investment funds (FCP) or as investment companies (SICAV or SICAF) and authorisations and routine approvals and supervision are the responsibility of the CSSF – *Commission de Surveillance du Secteur Financier.* In common with other centres, Luxembourg has updated its laws to align with the latest EU UCITS Directive and the *Law of 20 December* 2002 is now the current legislation governing managers and depositaries of UCITS schemes and SICAVs. Like Ireland, Luxembourg is primarily an administrative centre for funds that are targeted at investors elsewhere in Europe, but having been the first to capitalise on the UCITS Directive, Luxembourg has three to four times the value of funds under management than Dublin's IFSC and has currently pulled ahead of France for leadership of the European league table.

South Africa – the Collective Investment Schemes Control Act, which updated and replaced previously existing unit trust legislation, was enacted in 2002 and in place at the start of 2003. This Act moved legislation more in line with international best practice and was the subject of negotiation between the trade association and regulatory authorities for some years. The Financial Advisory and Intermediary Services Act (FAIS), which became law towards the end of 2002, had as its purpose the regulation of financial planners and advisers, as well as product suppliers, in the giving of advice and the conduct of their business in all areas where other industry legislation did not make specific provision. During its passage as a Bill, it had an impact in terms of how and what advisers were selling, in anticipation of the law. The

Financial Intelligence Centre Act, aimed at combating money-laundering activities, brought South Africa into line with international best practice and the subordinate legislation enabling effective practical implementation was in place by year-end 2002. In spite of its name, the Securities Services Act 2004 does not apply to collective investment schemes, nor to activities regulated under FAIS, and the Financial Markets Advisory Board, established by the Financial Markets Control Act 1989, continues.

Spain – a new Mutual Fund Law, the 'CIS Law' (35/2003), implemented the expansion of the UCITS Directive and effectively established hedge funds; prior to this, the principal legislation was the *Ley de Instituciones de Inversión Colectiva* of 1984 and the *Real Decreto de Instituciones de Inversión Colectiva* of 1990, amended in February 2001. Supervisory responsibility is vested in the CNMV – *Comisión Nacional del Mercado de Valores*, established by the Securities Market Law which was updated by Law 37/1998. Unusually, there are no institutional funds in Spain but this may change as CNMV's circular of 3 May 2006 issued rules for hedge funds.

These selected descriptions reveal both the origins and focus of regulation, as well as the extents to which self-regulation is permitted or encouraged, and to which regulation of securities businesses is carried out by a separate regulator or one with responsibility for the entire financial sector. As a sweeping generalisation, development in Asia began more as a government initiative to marshall capital versus the commercially-driven initiatives of the Western world. It is also interesting, salutary perhaps, to note that far and away the largest mutual fund nation in the world – the USA

– has operated under primary legislation that is now over 60 years old and has not concerned itself either with self-regulation or with combining the roles of separate industry regulators.

Nevertheless, without exception, responsibility for authorisation or licensing and prudential supervision of firms and individuals engaged in the business of funds management lies with a central, governmental agency or department. The authorisation of individual funds usually resides with this same agency, but the agency may or may not be responsible for supervising other businesses in the financial sector – banking or insurance for example. Indeed, setting and monitoring compliance with detailed operational and conduct of business rules that govern the day-to-day activities of firms may even be the responsibility of a self-regulatory organisation, sometimes working with or through trade associations.

Certainly all governments aim to control the promotion or marketing of funds to the general public, in order both to minimise the risk of fraud or of mis-selling to the most vulnerable sections of the community and to stimulate those same people to invest for their future retirement.

3.2 THE PROCESS OF AUTHORISATION

Once the sponsoring manager has obtained approval or authorisation to conduct its general investment business, the process of obtaining authorisation for its funds to be marketed to the general public follows a similar pattern in most countries. Documents which establish the company or trust – a deed of incorporation or a deed of trust – together with a prospectus or equivalent particulars of how the scheme will operate, are submitted together with a marketing plan, a fee and a formal request for authorisation to the relevant authority.

In addition to setting out the name and objectives of the mutual fund, the application needs to identify the key parties involved and, if applicable, provide details of their respective permissions or authorisations to conduct investment business. Regulations usually require a fund to have a manager and a custodian (Australia is an exception in this regard), but there may be others performing specialist tasks as investment adviser, registrar or transfer agent, auditor and administrator. Investment companies, of course, will also have directors and possibly other officers.

The regulator's process of screening applications includes:

- assessing whether all these parties are:
  - fit and proper for the roles they are to perform, and have adequate resources
  - sufficiently independent of each other;
- being satisfied that the aims and objectives of the mutual fund are permissible and achievable;
- being satisfied that the scheme is or will become a viable proposition.

The process of setting up a mutual fund may be viewed as costly and complicated, depending on the jurisdiction. In the USA, it has been assessed that a fund distributed in all States needs to reach an NAV of between $50 million to $100 million within a relatively short time if it is to be economically viable. Preparing the federal registration statement, contracts, state filings and corporate documents could cost $100,000 in legal fees, while filing fees themselves may exceed $30,000, to say nothing of printing costs of maybe $25,000 and the statutory requirement for the fund to have assets of $100,000 before distributing its shares to the public – money that usually has to be put up by the sponsor as 'seed capital'. The UK's FSA has a more moderate fee structure, at least for UK-domiciled funds – £1,200 to consider applications for a UCITS fund authorisation, £1,500 for non-UCITS retail schemes and £2,400 for Qualified Investor Schemes. For non-UK funds, the charge rises steeply to £14,000 however.

3.3 FUND MANAGEMENT

The investment management of a mutual fund's assets is subject to compliance with the aims and policies stated in the prospectus (or equivalent offering document or explanatory memorandum) and to limitations imposed by regulations or, if more constraining, by the terms of the fund's constituting deed or instrument of incorporation. This is the case if the investment management is carried out by the fund's own sponsoring manager or management company, or by a third party appointed under contract to be portfolio manager or investment adviser.

Investors must be protected from unexpected and undesired changes in the purpose and practices of their chosen investment vehicle. Regulations therefore impose both a fiduciary responsibility and prescriptive rules on the operators of mutual funds to ensure there are no unauthorised or imprudent dealings.

Normally, investment is restricted to transferable securities that are listed on a recognised stock exchange, and, for funds that are to be marketed to the general public, investment in gold, oil, sugar and other physical commodities is generally not permitted but investment in property may be. The details are examined more closely in Chapter 5, but the regulations usually reflect the general principles of collective investment, which are that the fund and its management should have the following characteristics:

Spread and diversification

The fund must operate on the principle of spreading risk, meaning that the portfolio must be invested in the securities of several issuers, with no single holding or category of holdings exceeding prescribed percentages of the total portfolio – 'the eggs must not all be in the same basket'.

This general rule, although sound, is limited in its effectiveness to mitigate risk, as it does not require diversification across geographic, economic or industrial sectors – indeed many authorised funds are funds that specialise or concentrate on investing in just one sector. Similarly, it is likely not to require diversification across different classes of asset, such as bonds, equities or property. The absence of such a requirement allows specialist funds to be established to invest wholly in Government securities, for example, or in technology stocks or physical property, or to concentrate on specific country or regional economies.

Nevertheless, even these funds are usually required to comply with the principal risk-spreading requirement to hold a number of different securities, including, for example, a Government securities fund required to hold a number of different issues of its chosen Government's stock, even though the entire portfolio may be stock issued by a single Government. Conversely, a fund specialising in property investment may be barred from being fully invested in physical property, for reasons of liquidity, and required to hold marketable securities issued by property companies to a given percentage.

A recent development in Europe via amendment to the UCITS Directive has been to allow (but not require) greater diversification across asset classes, such that previous prohibitions on mixing property with securities, for example, or restrictions on mixing direct investments with investments via funds of funds, have been lifted, or will be once Member States implement the terms of the Directive or make mandatory the new rules, as the UK has done for effect from February 2007.

Concentration/influence

No individual investment should be of such a size that it allows the fund to exercise significant or undue influence over the management or operation of the underlying business or exposes the fund unduly to the fortunes of the underlying business. Although, under principles of corporate governance, fund managers are quite understandably being encouraged to exercise their voting rights, their business is investment management not the running of the businesses they invest in. A common restriction is for a fund to be restricted to holding no more than 10% of the issued capital of a company it invests in.

Contingency cover

Underwritings, rights issues, convertible and partly-paid securities each create a contingent liability or asset. Most jurisdictions impose conditions on the extent to which a fund may hold such securities or enter into arrangements that could lead to securities being acquired or payments being called for. Normally, the fund can include such securities or rights or underwriting commitments, but only if the manager can demonstrate to the custodian's or trustee's satisfaction that, in the event of having to take up the underwriting, or the rights, or convert or make further payments on the securities, these actions could be undertaken from current resources and without the resultant portfolio breaching any of the governing regulations.

Use of derivatives

Use of derivatives, such as stock or currency futures, options or index contracts may be restricted to specialist funds or, if allowed for general funds, limited to specific types of transaction, which are non-speculative, such as for the covered hedging of portfolio risks. The EU's latest UCITS Directive goes further than previous fund regulations by allowing both exchange-traded and 'over-the-counter' (OTC) derivatives to be the main asset class of a fund, provided the manager has in place a sound risk management process. This relaxation of the restrictions on using derivatives allows the conventional 'long-only' fund to adopt strategies more common in the management of hedge funds.

Liquidity and borrowing

To ensure that investors can enjoy timely settlement when they redeem their shares or units and when they are due to benefit from other payment obligations imposed upon the manager, particularly the payment of income, it is crucial that an appropriate portion of a fund's assets can be held in cash or in securities that can be readily realised and converted into cash. Consequently, regulators tend to impose a restriction on the proportion of the portfolio that can be held in securities that are not listed on a recognised or approved exchange, or, as was noted above, in immovable assets such as property.

Conversely, regulations may require that the amount of liquid assets held in the fund's portfolio, such as uninvested cash or short-dated Government securities, is not excessive in relation to known or anticipated obligations, on the grounds, for example, that an equity fund should be invested in equities. The EU's latest UCITS Directive takes a different stance and reclassifies money market instruments and cash as permitted asset classes in their own right, rather than being ancillary liquid assets.

Generally, except to provide liquidity in well-specified circumstances, an open-ended fund is prohibited from borrowing, and even permitted borrowing must not be continuous. Closed-ended funds, which are typically exchange-traded companies, are, by contrast, often allowed to gear by structured borrowing through the issuing of debt securities. Unregulated funds are not subject to any such restrictions and may have an extremely high proportion of their assets funded by borrowings – hedge funds frequently are highly geared and introduce interest rate risk on top of security and market risk.

Generally, the various conditions described above must be met both at the time individual assets are acquired and throughout the life of the fund. To provide flexibility when price movements cause inadvertent breaches after acquisition, the manager may be offered a period of time to achieve correction; six months is normally allowed in Europe, for example.

Finally, regulations may require that before personnel may engage in fund portfolio management without supervision, they must have acquired a demonstrable level of knowledge and competence by way of examinations passed and observed records of achievement in carrying out the function while under supervision.

3.4 MARKETING

The extent to which funds can be marketed within a state or country or across state or national borders varies from country to country and depends on local laws and the nature of any federation or other affiliation which determines where the ultimate authority lies.

Most jurisdictions permit the marketing of mutual funds, but the only funds they will allow to be marketed freely are those they have authorised or which have been authorised by a federated or affiliated jurisdiction as eligible for marketing or promotion to the general public and registered as such. The marketing of other funds or securities will be either prohibited or restricted to promotion to professional or institutional investors only.

The prospectus

The documents submitted to the regulator when seeking authorisation or registration include a comprehensive disclosure document – the *prospectus*. This must meet prescribed requirements regarding the form and content and, after authorisation, be offered or supplied to each prospective investor. Investors must be supplied with current information concerning the operation and performance of a fund and so rules governing disclosure of information are usually in addition to, and separate from, those governing content and registration of the initial prospectus.

This is especially relevant with respect to promotional advertisements and particularly if it is permissible to solicit investment 'off-the-page'. Practice varies: for example, off-the-page advertisements are prohibited in the US, whereas they are allowed by UK authorities. However, all jurisdictions seek to regulate the type, form and content of investment advertisements and have specific rules governing advertisements of or by mutual funds, including nowadays, promotion and investment via the Internet.

A further aspect of regulation concerns the employment by the fund of salesmen or by investors of independent advisers. In either case, most jurisdictions impose requirements that salesmen and advisers are demonstrably competent to perform the function for which they are employed. Again, practice varies but to be approved or licensed, an adviser must generally present:

- a combination of formal written examinations;
- observed and recorded performance 'on the job' against pre-set criteria;
- continuing professional development or training.

These topics are covered in greater detail in Chapter 6.

3.5 ADMINISTRATION

The *administration* of a mutual fund extends to all areas of its operation, including fund management and marketing discussed above. However, the term is more usually applied to the 'back office' procedures, including the accounting and reporting associated with:

- buying and selling of securities comprising the investment portfolio;
- receipt, custody and delivery of securities and associated settlement payments;
- collection of income arising from holding securities;
- valuation of holdings and other assets and liabilities to determine fund dealing prices;
- creating, cancelling, issuing and redeeming of shares or units and associated charges and payments;
- maintaining a register of holders;
- dealing with complaints, errors and breaches of regulations;
- allocating income and its distribution to or accumulation on behalf of holders;
- paying fees, charges, taxes and other expenses arising from operation of the fund;
- keeping investors informed about the activity, standing and performance of the fund;
- organising and holding annual general meetings and extraordinary meetings of holders to approve changes in constitution or operation of the fund;
- ensuring adequate resources and controls (physical and financial) and regulatory compliance, including

maintenance of records, written procedures and fund documents.

Each of these topics is typically the subject of some regulation and is covered in more detail in Chapter 7. Management companies must demonstrate sound administration capabilities alongside investment skills and financial resources to be considered *fit and proper* to operate an authorised mutual fund.

The purpose of such wide-ranging regulation is to ensure that the interests of investors are protected as far as possible and appropriate throughout the life-cycle of their investment:

- at entry into the fund;
- whilst holding shares or units in the fund;
- upon exit from the fund,

against unscrupulous or incompetent managers or maladministration. Protection in these respects is not protection against loss caused by poor choice of fund or by market movements – investors must retain responsibility for their own investment judgement!

The regulations also seek to ensure as far as is possible that all investors are treated fairly in relation to each other. For example, the price paid by incoming investors or to outgoing investors should not be set at too high or too low a level such that its use dilutes the interests of the existing or continuing holders. Restrictions are also imposed upon the manager and other parties involved with the operation of the fund to ensure that they gain no special advantage from their dealings with the fund or with each other.

Regulation is enforced by a variety of means, including:

- periodic inspection visits by the regulator and the custodian or trustee;
- filings of reports, accounts and investment and tax returns;
- annual audits by independent auditors;
- occasionally, by the actions of vigilant shareholders.

3.6 INVESTOR PROTECTION

No amount of regulation will protect the foolish investor nor will it eliminate fraudsters. However, sensible regulation coupled with focused monitoring and informed alert investors:

- enhances the reputations of the world's investment industries;
- increases the involvement of ordinary individuals in investment; and
- improves the opportunities for Governments and commercial enterprises to foster economic growth.

The categories of activity in which regulations seek to provide investor protection can be summarised as follows:

Solvency

The various parties involved in the management and operation of a mutual fund must demonstrate they have and can maintain a continuing level of capital adequacy – minimum overall financial resources and liquid capital – so that they can withstand setbacks and continue in business in spite of losses or reduced income when markets fall or when their funds experience net redemptions by investors.

Independence

The parties involved in the operation and management of a fund must demonstrate and maintain a proper degree of independence from each other. Dealings with the fund must be at 'arm's length' terms and the management and custody of assets must be clearly separated, with the exception already noted of Australia, which has introduced the concept of the 'single responsible entity'.

Competence

All parties must ensure the current and continuing competence of their systems and personnel, including senior management, to carry out their respective functions and comply with all applicable regulations governing investment, marketing and administration. Regulators increasingly require the registration of key personnel.

Communications

- promotional material must be clear, fair and not misleading;
- prospectuses or similar must be complete, accurate and readily available for supply or inquiry;
- contract notes or similar confirmations of transactions must be issued promptly and contain prescribed information;
- periodic statements, accounts and other reports must be issued regularly and within prescribed timescales;
- meetings must be held to approve material changes before they can be put into effect.

Cancellation and compensation

Additionally, investors may have the benefit of:

- cancellation rights (or a 'cooling-off' period), if they agreed to invest as a result of the admonitions of an adviser or salesman;
- defined complaints procedures;
- compensation schemes, entitling them to compensation from a central fund in the event of the failure of the advising or providing company proven guilty of dishonesty, malpractice or other abuse.

Further protection is offered by way of regular inspection and monitoring by the regulators and the threat – for management companies – of fines and withdrawal of authority to conduct business.

Market abuse and insider dealing

Most jurisdictions have enacted some form of legislation, regulation or code of conduct to prohibit any individual or group of individuals from making a profit by the use of inside information or by any other method, whereby their securities dealings or their behaviour creates a false market, whether by price distortion or otherwise.

Money laundering

Through worldwide cooperation, governments impose obligations on management companies and their employees to carry out verification checks on the identity of investors and the source of their funds. This is to prevent *money laundering*, which is the process of converting *dirty money* gained from illegal activity into clean money by integrating it into the legitimate economy, e.g., by buying then selling investments.

Pricing

Regulators typically expect that managers will calculate the buying and selling prices of units in their funds based on each particular fund's net asset value (NAV) divided by the total number of units in issue. In arriving at the NAV, regulations may prescribe how each asset type is to be valued or they may simply require the manager to describe the valuation bases and process in scheme documents and apply them consistently and fairly. Either way, the aim is that investors are treated fairly and that the price applied to each transaction neither favours nor disadvantages incoming, outgoing or continuing holders.

Chapter

4

....

CONSTITUTION AND CONSTRAINTS

This chapter looks at the practical steps and documents required to set up a mutual fund. Day-to-day management and administration of the fund's capital and income is described, followed by termination or winding-up procedures and the charges paid by investors.

4.1 ESTABLISHMENT, SET-UP AND CHANGES

Establishment

Establishing a mutual fund follows a similar procedure in all countries. First, a management company determines the investment opportunity for a fund with a particular investment objective and policy, then decides its appropriate type or construction, either the corporate type, as an investment company, or the contractual type, as a unit or investment trust. It is worth noting that, in law, only the corporate type has a 'legal personality'.

Usually in conjunction with an independent custodian, depositary or trustee, the fund's constitutional documents are prepared and executed as legally binding instruments. The officers and agents, such as the investment manager, transfer agent, selling agent, administrator, auditor, are identified and then the terms and conditions upon which the fund will be offered and operated are settled and the charges and fees of the various parties agreed. Application for authorisation is then made to the relevant authority.

Depending on the jurisdiction, authorisation of the management company and the other parties concerned either precedes any application for authorisation of the mutual fund, or it is carried out as a single process when the management company first makes application for authorisation of a fund. Either way, the fund does not become authorised until the regulators are satisfied that it and the parties involved meet certain minimum requirements along the following lines:

• the management company must have a minimum capitalisation and 'free resources' sufficient to fund its expenses for, say, three or six months;
• except in Australia, the custodian, depositary or trustee must be independent of the management company and have a minimum capitalisation, which typically is substantially greater than that required for the management company. In Hong Kong, for example, HK$1 million is the management company requirement, but for the custodian/trustee it is HK$10 million;
• the management company (and any separate investment manager) must have appropriately qualified and experienced personnel engaged in the fund's management and administration. In the US and UK, compulsory training and competence schemes have had to be operated by management companies for personnel engaged in portfolio management or administration and in selling or advising on investments for some years and this form of requirement is gradually being imposed throughout the world;
• the fund itself must meet certain operational requirements set out in the relevant regulations

dealing with matters such as frequency of valuation and dealing, calculation of NAV and unit prices, publication of prices and other information, maintenance of shareholder records, and controls over transactions with connected persons;

- the fund must also meet various investment requirements applicable to its objectives or fund type, including diversification, concentration, liquidity, limits on the use of derivatives and on borrowing;
- to allow investors to make informed decisions, detailed disclosure requirements must be adhered to by the fund;
- if the fund has been authorised in another jurisdiction, or the management company is not resident in the country concerned, then it must have a resident licensed representative with whom investors can deal.

The method by which the fund meets these requirements is set out in its prospectus, which, together with the instrument of incorporation (or the trust deed) and appropriate fee, must accompany submission of a completed application form to the central regulator. Other information may be required, such as:

- a marketing plan, including sales projections for, say, three years and a statement of how quickly the fund is expected to become viable;
- the management company's latest audited accounts and personal details of its directors and senior officers;
- the custodian's or trustee's latest audited accounts and consent to appointment;

- if the fund has been authorised in another jurisdiction, evidence of authorisation and, if already up and running, its most recent audited report and accounts.

If any of these documents is not in the local language or another acceptable or official language, it may have to be supplied in a translation.

If the regulators are satisfied, an order of authorisation is issued and the fund may commence operations in that country. The process may take between 15 days and six weeks, depending on whether the parties involved are already approved and whether the fund is of a standard type.

Set-up

Set-up involves the putting in place of staff, systems and procedures to deal with the business of operating the fund or enhancing existing resources to deal with an additional fund. A fund in the form of a company may be the owner of these resources itself but a trust typically cannot own 'fixed assets' or other physical resources. The company can usually recover the costs of these resources from operation of the fund by writing off the original outlay on set-up, possibly over a number of years (known as '*amortisation*') but more typically in the first year, and, if an umbrella structure is established, by spreading the write-off over a number of sub-funds. Annual running costs are covered by charges made on the issue of shares and management of the fund.

Where the fund is not self-managed, which is the case usually with the contractual type or trust, then set-up and its costs fall to the management company and its appointed administrators and transfer agents. The management company is entitled to charge fees for its services and, in turn, can contract with its agents to pay for their services, either from its own income or, if the regulations permit, directly from the fund.

Once set-up is complete, marketing can begin (see Chapter 6). When sufficient shares are sold, the fund can begin its investment programme, the activity generally understood as 'fund management' (see Chapter 5).

Changes

Once the fund is up and running, any *changes* to the details supplied to the regulators when applying for authorisation must be referred back for approval if they amount to a material change. Extreme examples would be seeking to operate a fund authorised as a bond fund as an equity fund, an America fund as a Japan fund, but 'material' also means changes to the maximum rates of fees or charges that can be borne by the fund or charged to investors or changes in the investment objectives, for example, from capital growth to high income.

The approval process typically includes gaining the approval of shareholders in *general meeting* (see Chapter 7). This is mandatory for certain proposed changes and otherwise if the trustee/custodian believes it to be necessary.

Some changes can be made without such approval, although notice of change is usually required. For example, the maximum rate of a particular charge may be laid down in scheme documents. A proposal to increase this rate requires prior approval, but a proposal to increase the currently applied rate to a rate that does not exceed the maximum could be implemented after giving notice to shareholders. In the UK, for example, the notice period is 90 days.

4.2 SCHEME DOCUMENTS

For regulatory purposes, there are two essential scheme documents:

* the instrument of incorporation (if a company) or the trust deed (if a trust);
* the prospectus or offering document, also known in some jurisdictions as *scheme particulars.*

It is the *instrument of incorporation* that establishes the mutual fund, and a fund established as a company may well have a *certificate of incorporation* before it applies for authorisation. However, it cannot be offered to the public until it has an *order of authorisation.*

Other documents include the regular reports issued by the fund or its manager in accordance with regulatory requirements (see Chapter 7) and, if the fund is listed on a stock exchange, the *listing notice.*

Instrument of incorporation

This is a publicly available document that must be filed along with other material before the fund can be launched. Regulations prescribe what it must contain and, whether it is the Memorandum and Articles for a company or a deed for a trust, the minimum contents usually are:

- name, type, size and currency of fund;
- names and official addresses of the promoters (manager, custodian/trustee);
- country of incorporation and governing law;
- a provision that share- or unit holders' liability to make payments is limited to the amount payable for the purchase of shares or units;
- duration of the fund if it is to terminate at some future date;
- authority for charges to be levied and the maximum rates of those charges;
- restrictions on how the fund may be invested;
- whether different classes of share or type of unit may be issued and a description of each;
- if the fund is only to be held by certain types of investor, a statement to that effect;
- provisions covering the issue or non-issue of registered or bearer certificates;
- other provisions required to enable the fund to pursue its purpose or included as a restatement of applicable statutory provisions, such as permitted investments, power of manager to be a holder, procedures for meetings and for termination.

Prospectus

A *prospectus* is a legal document intended to provide potential investors with important information about the fund. There are stiff penalties for including misleading or inaccurate statements and for omissions. Investors use and may rely upon this information when deciding whether to invest in the fund. It is the manager's responsibility to provide a prospectus to the investor, but the investor's responsibility to read it.

The prospectus must be dated and reviewed and updated periodically, usually at least annually. Usual contents repeat some matters contained in the instrument of incorporation (or deed or *company prospectus*) and include:

- detailed information about the manager, custodian/ trustee, investment adviser, auditor, registrar/transfer agent and how each may be contacted;
- name, type and date of establishment of the fund, and, if a company, its capital structure, and if a trust, its unit types;
- investment objectives, policies, restrictions and risks;
- how shares or units may be bought or sold, any maximum or minimum for the amount of investment or holding, how unit prices are determined, and what charges are levied upon entry or exit;
- what charges may be levied upon the fund, how they are computed and the maximum and minimum amounts or rates if applicable;

- the accounting date of the fund, the accounting periods for reporting purposes, and the dates and frequency of reports;
- when and how net income will be allocated and distributed to holders;
- general descriptions of the taxation of the fund and of investors;
- what matters require holders' approval and procedures for meetings and voting;
- descriptions of circumstances when dealings may be suspended;
- procedure for termination or winding-up;
- any other information that ought reasonably to be included to enable investors to make informed decisions.

4.3 LAUNCH PROCEDURES AND PRACTICES

Once a mutual fund is authorised, it is launched to potential investors by way of an initial offer of shares or units at a fixed price. The terms of the offer are restricted by regulations, which cover matters such as how long the initial offer period may last and the circumstances that require it to close.

The fund or its management company may set a minimum and a maximum target of capital to be raised, and the prospectus must explain what will happen if those targets are not reached or are exceeded.

The launch is usually accomplished by making announcements in the press, mailings to prospective investors, launch briefings for advisers and agents, and advertisements. Although not permitted in the US, some countries allow advertisements to solicit money 'off the page' by inclusion of an application form. Nowadays, this extends to advertising and making investment via the Internet.

During the period of the initial offer, the fund does not normally invest subscriptions received from would-be share- or unit holders, but waits to see how much has been raised and whether this exceeds the minimum or maximum amount specified in the offering prospectus. Some jurisdictions allow investment prior to close of the offer period, but only if this possibility is stated in the prospectus and has been agreed with the custodian or trustee. In this case, it is usual to require the NAV to be kept under review and, if it would create a share or unit price materially different from the fixed offer price, for the offer to close and the fund to move to the normal NAV basis of dealing. In the UK, the relevant difference is plus or minus 2% from the fixed price.

4.4 RUNNING THE FUND

Running the fund can be thought of in terms of management, marketing and administration, and each of these functions is described in detail in Chapters 5, 6 and 7.

Each function has to distinguish between *capital* and *income* to some extent:

Capital

Management is concerned essentially with investment management and initially with investment of the capital raised from the launch of the fund. The investment objectives of the fund determine the type of security and specific investments, but unless the fund is promoted as concentrating on producing a stated or implied income yield, the manager will structure the fund's portfolio so as to preserve and enhance its capital value.

Marketing the fund requires, among other things, an explanation of the investment objectives and policies and how policies and charges may affect the security and growth of capital.

Administration requires the accurate and complete recording of capital transactions and positions for purposes of settlement/delivery, valuation, reporting, taxation and reconciliations with the custodian's records.

Income

Depending on the jurisdiction, income may include realised capital gains, but normally it refers to the income arising from holding assets acquired as a result of deploying the capital, such as dividends and interest. Strictly, the term should be *net income*, as almost invariably it is meant to convey the income after expenses, charges and taxation.

Management is concerned with income to the extent that the fund's objectives include achieving a particular level or rate of income. Fund managers have a variety of techniques and instruments available to them to improve the level of income (including the charging of certain expenses to capital), but must balance the drive for income with the risk of reducing the quality and capital growth prospects of the underlying portfolio. High-yielding equities frequently carry greater risk, whilst high-yielding corporate or Government bonds carry little prospect of capital growth in a stable interest rate environment. Charging expenses to capital may inhibit capital growth or, in extreme circumstances, actually erode capital.

Marketing the fund must include an explanation of the likely income yield and, if a bond fund, the yield to redemption, as well as the bases and effect of charges, and the policies and practices for allocation and distribution or reinvestment of net income.

Administration involves collecting the income (usually a responsibility of the custodian or trustee) and paying the expenses, charges and taxes. Detailed records of income must be kept to verify that:

- all entitlements are received;
- only permitted expenses are paid;
- net income available for allocation to individual share- or unit holders can be determined with confidence, distributed accurately and reported on as required.

4.5 CHARGES

Several charges are associated with mutual funds, although they need not all apply to every fund. Charges are the costs that investors pay for the administration and management of their investment, applied in one of three ways:

- as part of the share or unit price paid upon entry to the fund;
- as a direct charge rendered separately from the amount of the investment;
- paid from the property (assets) of the fund.

In most countries, the regulations will seek to ensure that excessive charges are not levied and will require fund managers to disclose both the current and maximum rates of their charges, how they are calculated and applied, and generally require that they are fairly and clearly explained to potential investors.

Front-end, sales, initial or preliminary charge

This may be imposed when an investor buys shares or units, and is often included in the price. It is intended to cover the costs of marketing the fund, such as advertising, promotional mailing and commission paid to sales agents or intermediaries.

In the UK, this charge can be quite high by comparison to other jurisdictions (as much as 5% or up to 7% of the amount invested in an equities fund, but considerably lower for a bond or money market fund) but, as elsewhere, and particularly in the USA, competition in the investment industry has given impetus to a trend for 'no-load' funds, where front-end charges are reduced or abandoned.

Dealing commission

If the investment is bought or sold through a stock exchange, the stockbroker will charge a normal commission.

Annual, periodic or management charge

This is the principal income of the management company and is usually paid from the property of the fund, spread over the year and based on the value (NAV) of the fund. It covers the management company's costs of investment management and administration, and is typically between ¾% and 2% pa, varying according to the type of fund.

Withdrawal, exit or redemption charge

The withdrawal charge (also known as an exit or redemption fee or charge) may be applied when all or part of the investment is sold, instead of, or in combination with, the initial charge. Its purpose is to encourage investors to remain invested for a reasonable period or, put another way, to discourage early redemption. It is often imposed according to a sliding scale, for example:

Sell within (years)	Charge
1	5%
2	4%
3	3%
4	2%
5	1%
5+	none

Third parties' fees

If a custodian, depositary or trustee is required to safeguard the property of the fund, they will charge fees that are paid from the fund or by the manager. Similarly, in some countries a registrar's or transfer agent's fee is paid to the company that maintains the register of share- or unit holders.

Commission and other charges

Some fund managers sell their products through intermediaries, and pay *commission*. This is not an extra cost to the investor, but is either absorbed by the manager or covered by the initial charge. Some intermediaries waive this commission to increase their client's investment, preferring to charge fees to their client instead. The maximum rate of commission and its disclosure are both subject to regulation in many countries. Other charges may include amortisation of set-up costs and of any immovable assets (e.g. office buildings) owned by the fund.

4.6 TERMINATION/WINDING-UP

Termination and *winding-up* applies to all funds with a fixed termination date or a stated duration and in certain circumstances to other funds or the sub-funds of umbrella funds.

Whilst some of today's mutual funds have been in existence for 50 or more years, at some point all funds face the prospect of termination, either because falling investor interest leads to mass redemptions, making the fund uneconomic to operate, or because changes in the investment or economic environment make the investment objective unattractive or unachievable, making it extremely difficult to attract new investors. In such cases, the manager may be permitted to apply to the regulator for the fund's authorisation to be revoked on the grounds that its continued operation is no longer commercially viable, and for it to be wound up or terminated.

Merging or amalgamating one fund or sub-fund with another may seem like an alternative to termination, and it is, from the point of view of participants who wish to continue with some form of investment. From a legal standpoint, however, mergers usually involve one or both of the subject funds being discontinued, or terminated, with the other or a new fund acquiring the assets of the discontinuing fund(s). Regulations usually set out both the circumstances and the procedures for a termination, including winding-up the fund and distributing its remaining assets. Winding-up is usually a voluntary action, but there are circumstances where winding-up is compulsory, including:

- withdrawal of the fund's order of authorisation for any reason;
- expiration of the period for which the fund was established and authorised;
- approval of an amalgamation, merger or allocation of its assets with or to one or more other funds.

The manner of a winding-up may depend upon the terms of any scheme of merger or amalgamation approved by the fund's share- or unit holders, but otherwise normally proceeds as follows:

- dealings in the fund's shares or units are suspended and participants and relevant regulators notified;
- if the fund is a company, a liquidator is appointed to supervise and control its liquidation and to instruct the custodian or trustee;
- the custodian or trustee realises the net assets of the fund, and either the liquidator or the trustee pays off or makes provision for any remaining liabilities, including the costs of winding-up, and then distributes the net proceeds to remaining participants in proportion to their share- or unit holdings;

- any unclaimed net proceeds or other cash (including any unclaimed income distributions) held by the liquidator/trustee at the time the fund is finally dissolved will have to be dealt with according to the governing law, which may require that such amounts are paid over to the courts for safekeeping or disbursement.

When the winding-up is completed, the relevant regulator(s) are informed and the formalities completed by withdrawal or revocation of the order of authorisation.

Provided the process of winding-up is completed within a reasonably short time, reports and accounts are usually required only upon dissolution and sent to each person who was a participant immediately before the date of dissolution.

Chapter
5

....

FUND
MANAGEMENT

This chapter shows how different investment policies and strategies are used to achieve the investment objectives of a mutual fund. The restrictions on investment imposed by regulations and the construction of the fund are described together with the effect of borrowing and gearing.

5.1 INVESTMENT POLICIES AND OBJECTIVES

Each mutual fund has one or more investment objectives. For example, to provide an above-average and increasing income and a yield about 50% higher than the relevant index. It is the investment manager's task to achieve these objectives, by pursuing a stated investment policy. Each investment management company will adopt an appropriate policy for each of its funds but will tend to have an overall 'house style' or strategy. Two contrasting approaches are:

- 'Bottom-up'. Known as *stock-picking*. The manager looks for outstanding individual companies. They can be identified from research reports or from personal knowledge of their products, services and management.
- 'Top-down'. Starts with *asset allocation*. The manager reviews world or national economy trends first, determines his *asset allocation model* in terms of geographic and industrial spread, then examines industries in detail and finally selects companies that will benefit from the trends.

Another contrast in styles between different houses is between *passive* and *active* management.

Passive management occurs when portfolio changes are made only in response to changes in specific external references, such as the components and value of index constituents. The performance of most funds is compared with an appropriate index. A passive policy will seek to emulate or match the index movement, either by replicating the index stocks within the fund's portfolio or by holding, say, 60% of the fund in the major constituents only and investing the rest in derivative instruments that model the balance of the index. The performance of the fund should move in line, both up and down, with the index. Such funds are also known as *tracker funds* and the extent to which they do not match the index performance is called the *tracking error*.

An active or aggressive policy involves changes to the portfolio based upon the manager's judgement after detailed research and assessment, and aims to outperform the relevant index, rising faster or falling more slowly.

5.2 INVESTMENT RESTRICTIONS

Regulations impose a number of *restrictions* or constraints on the types and amount of investment that can be held by a mutual fund, and the scheme documentation may contain further limitations that cannot be breached by the investment manager. Regulations usually will specify also that the investment objectives and policy as set out in scheme documents cannot be changed materially without approval by vote of the share- or unit holders.

Consistency with investment objectives and type of fund

The investment manager must select investments that are consistent with the investment objectives of the fund, which may be reflected in the name of the fund, indicating the fund's purpose or the type of assets it will hold. For example, for an equity fund with the objective of capital growth from investing in Japanese smaller companies, the selection of American money market instruments would not be acceptable. To minimise the strictures of such regulations, the objective, or more usually, the policy, may be framed with a flexibility that is indicated in the name of the fund – for example, 'Asia-Pacific' or 'Japan and General' would allow investment in Japanese and other countries' companies.

Spread of risk and diversification

Regulatory constraints to ensure that authorised funds hold a sufficient spread of investments to dilute the effect of failure of any one are a fundamental requirement. While general requirements can be applied to all types of fund, more exact requirements need to be developed to suit different types of mutual fund, particularly as regards the chosen asset class. With the advent of the 'mixed fund', the broad classifications of funds as 'equity funds', 'stock funds', 'money funds', 'fund of funds', and so on has diminished relevance but, as an example, prior to adoption of the EU's latest UCITS Directive, the UK's FSA defined nine types of fund:

- securities funds – invest in equities and/or bonds, including Government or other public securities;
- money market funds – invest in cash and near cash, bills of exchange and debentures;
- futures and options funds and geared futures and options funds – invest in derivatives;
- property funds – invest directly in buildings and other real estate and property company shares;
- warrant funds – invest in warrants, which give the holder the right to subscribe for shares in a company during a specified period;
- feeder funds – pension schemes linked to a single unit trust;
- fund of funds – invests only in other funds;
- umbrella funds – a single scheme with any number of constituent parts or sub-funds providing the facility for holders to switch all or part of their investment from one sub-fund to another.

These classifications came about in order that the regulator could specify particular limits or restrictions appropriate to the type of fund rather than to all funds generally. Consequently, they are not to be confused with 'performance categories' defined by trade bodies to group funds with similar objectives or policies, even though there may be some overlap. Equally, the US *hybrid fund* should not be thought of as a truly *mixed fund* – it is a fund that holds a mixture of equities and bonds but not other asset classes.

Having specified general requirements for all funds, the FSA laid down further specific requirements for each of the nine types of fund. For example, those for a securities fund included:

- not more than 10% of the fund to be invested in unlisted securities – those not traded on a stock exchange;
- not more than 5% of the fund to be invested in other collective investment schemes;
- with the exception of Government securities, not more than 10% of the fund to be invested in any security, and the aggregate of all those exceeding 5% not to exceed 40%;
- up to 35% of the fund could be invested in Government and equivalent public corporation stocks, unless the trust deed permitted a higher figure;
- except for cash held for liquidity or other ancillary purposes, the fund to be wholly invested in freely transferable securities.

One effect of these restrictions was that a UK securities fund investing in equities had to hold at least 16 different investments – 4 at 10% (40%) and 12 at 5% (60%). In fact, most such funds held between 50 and 100 investments. Most of these restrictions have been carried forward into the newly-defined *UCITS Schemes*, although greater investment than previously allowed may be made in other collective investment schemes, in deposits and other money-market instruments, and, for tracker funds, in individual securities whose value exceeds 10% of the chosen index.

In the US, mutual funds belong to a class of investment companies defined in the Investment Company Act as 'management companies', which are further classified as being 'diversified' or 'non-diversified'. To qualify as a diversified company, the mutual fund must have at least 75% of its total assets represented by cash and near-cash items, Government securities, securities of other investment companies, and other securities, with not more than 5% in the securities of any one issuer, and not more than 10% of the voting securities of any one corporation. Generally speaking, a mutual fund meeting these criteria qualifies as a 'regulated investment company' (RIC) under the Internal Revenue Code of 1986 and does not have to account for tax on its operations, provided it distributes substantially all of its income to participating shareholders.

Although most investment managers will invest substantially all the fund's resources in the chosen asset classes, there is usually some amount uninvested, held in cash to meet possible redemption liabilities or as a provision for taking up new investment opportunities. For larger funds this could be, at any one time, a considerable sum – 3% to 5% of the value of the fund is not untypical, and 5% of $100m is $5,000,000. The manager and custodian or trustee will agree a procedure, whereby uninvested cash, excluding amounts placed by the manager into specific money-market instruments, is automatically held in interest-bearing short-term deposits, and will review the market from time to time to ensure that the optimum interest rate is obtained.

5.3 BORROWING AND GEARING

Regulations typically impose restrictions on a mutual fund borrowing money to 'gear up' its portfolio. In the UK, borrowing by an authorised open-ended fund must be temporary and limited to 10% of the value of the fund. Back-to-back loans for currency hedging purposes are excluded from this limit and, similarly for property funds, mortgages do not count as borrowing. Listed investment trusts are not subject to this restriction and may well have borrowing in the form of debt capital.

5.4 UNDERWRITING

Mutual funds may enter into underwriting agreements for securities that are to be issued, for example by way of an initial public offering (IPO). The reward is underwriting commission, which, although a small percentage, say ¼%, can be a source of additional income for the fund. Additionally, if the issue is not fully taken up by the public, underwriting also provides an opportunity to acquire shares that meet the investment objective of the fund without the usual dealing costs of market acquisition. Regulators typically limit a fund's ability to engage in underwriting to issues and amounts that the fund could hold under its regulations governing investment powers and limits.

5.5 STOCKLENDING

Mutual funds are generally managed as 'long-only' funds, i.e. short positions are not allowed. However, funds such as hedge funds and other investors who adopt a short-selling strategy need to borrow or otherwise acquire stock to cover their settlement obligations and may look to the trustees or custodians of mutual funds for that purpose. Provided the mutual fund's constitutional documents permit stocklending, it may enter into such an arrangement in exchange for a fee.

Chapter

6

....

MARKETING

This chapter explains that in most international markets a mutual fund can only be promoted to the public by authorised persons. International and cross-border constraints and the different distribution channels (the ways of promoting and marketing) are discussed.

6.1 AUTHORISATION

In most countries marketing of mutual funds to the general public is permitted, but only of funds that have been authorised or recognised by the jurisdiction, or by a federated or affiliated jurisdiction (see Chapter 3). Even so, it may be possible to promote unauthorised funds to professional and institutional investors, or to people no longer living in the country (expatriates).

6.2 CROSS-BORDER/ INTERNATIONAL MARKETING

The advent of the Internet has posed as much of a challenge to regulators as it has provided opportunities to fund management companies and their selling agents, but *restraints* on international marketing include:

Regulations

Regulations usually require that a mutual fund be authorised before it can be promoted to the public. Authorisation procedures include the submission of the prospectus or scheme particulars, which must meet prescribed requirements of form and content. The investment objectives of the fund also have to comply with the domestic standards of the country into which the fund is to be marketed.

Language

The prospectus or scheme particulars and other documentation will have to be provided in the principal language of the country in which it is to be marketed, and possibly other languages spoken widely in that country. As a separate matter, anti-discrimination legislation may well require that fund documents be available in large-size type, in Braille or in audio format.

Advertisements

Advertisements and other promotional material must comply with local regulations and conduct of business rules. Local advertising standards and regulations in each country may differ from the 'home state' rules and require, for instance, that certain specific details are contained in (or excluded from) advertisements. It may also be necessary to demonstrate that compliance checks have been completed.

Investment traditions

Some countries' investors may have a tradition of investing in a particular way, and be reluctant to change, whether to a new form or method of investing or to a new type of investment or to an investment managed by a 'foreigner'. In Germany, for instance, it is only recently that investors have begun to invest directly in equities, as distinct from bonds issued by banks who were the holders of direct equity.

These and many other restraints on international marketing can be overcome, or transformed into *opportunities*. Communication links around the world are improving all the time; the Internet in particular is now used to promote mutual funds, and information about them is therefore accessible from almost anywhere. The standardisation of the form of the mutual fund, the gradual simplification of its structure and a clear presentation of investment objectives, risks and management charges are all contributing to a better understanding of the product, which in turn is leading more investors to choose mutual funds to meet their own personal investment objectives.

6.3 DISTRIBUTION CHANNELS

Shares in mutual funds can be sold directly by the fund or by its management company to investors, or through agents employed by the fund or management company as sales agents or representatives in a sales force. Managers may also sell funds through independent intermediaries acting either as agents for their clients or simply as selling agents who employ consultants to provide advice and support but selling directly to the public.

In the US, mutual funds typically sell their shares through a separate organisation known as a *principal underwriter* or *distributor,* and only in a few instances will the fund sell its own shares. The independent intermediaries are usually firms set up as broker-dealers.

Sales force

The sales force comprises individual employees of the management company trained as salespeople whose job it is to persuade potential investors to use their company's products. Many countries have regulations that seek to set standards for conduct, and, in relation to advice, require that it is based on an understanding of the investors' circumstances and be suitable in relation to the investors' objectives and personal as well as financial circumstances. Accordingly, the salespeople should be suitably and adequately qualified and be required to demonstrate ongoing professional competence, development and training.

Companies that employ a sales force can be subjected to a considerable overhead arising from the regulatory requirements, which may require them to:

• document recruitment procedures and check references and qualifications;
• operate a training and competence scheme for experienced as well as for trainee staff;
• maintain ongoing training records;
• accommodate visits by the regulator's compliance inspectors, to check that procedures are documented

and carried out, and that records are properly maintained.

Intermediaries

An *intermediary* is a person, partnership or company who acts as an agent, either for one or several mutual fund management companies (in which case they are known as a *tied agent*) or for their clients on a professional advisory basis (in which case they are independent of any particular product provider). Unlike the tied (to one) or multi-tied (to several) management companies, the independent (or 'whole of market') intermediary may sell the funds of any management company, according to their clients' needs.

The regulatory requirements of intermediaries are similar to those for a sales force. The individual intermediary must also disclose whether he or she is tied, and what commission, if any, he or she will receive.

Direct promotion

Mutual funds can sell the shares or units and related products directly, using:

- advertisements on billboards, television, the Internet and in the press;
- other promotional items in newspapers and magazines;
- direct mailings;

- telephone sales;
- general publicity material;
- trade shows and conferences;
- sales offices;
- an interactive web-site.

The costs of such campaigns can be considerable, so the manager will set a response target, and may adjust the details of the campaign if progress is not satisfactory. Sometimes a special *discount* is offered to investors, especially for larger investments. The end of the financial or tax year is often a key time for attracting investors, particularly if the product has tax benefits or investment allowances related to individual fiscal years.

Marketing campaigns often combine more than one of the channels or direct methods and considerable thought will be given to each.

Considerations when using advertisements include:

- Which *publications* to use – different newspapers or journals have different types of reader. For example, the more serious papers with informed financial comment might be a suitable vehicle for attracting lump sum investments, whereas the tabloids may be appropriate for attracting smaller but regular contributions to a savings scheme.
- *'House' style* – a consistent style of advertisement helps towards name awareness. A company logo or

symbol, together with a consistent use of colour or type styles, is often used.

- *Costs* – advertising space can be expensive, but there may be discounts for repeated insertions, and specialist agencies may be able to negotiate favourable prices that justify their fees.
- *Media* – as well as newspapers and magazines, advertisements appear on television and radio, and on the Internet.
- *Regulations and advertising standards* – the contents of an advertisement may be constrained by regulations and other standards. For example:
  - it must be clear, fair and not misleading;
  - it must include a risk warning that the value of the investment may fall as well as rise;
  - it must include a warning that past performance is not necessarily a guide to future performance;
  - if performance is compared to that of an index, the basis of comparison must be consistent with the basis on which the index is constructed;
  - comparisons or statements of performance must not be selective but must show figures for a given period, perhaps the last five years.

Regulations may also require that advertisements are issued only by authorised persons, who maintain evidence that, prior to issue, the advertisement has been checked for compliance with regulations.

Other considerations when contemplating alternatives to direct advertising:

- *Other items in newspapers and magazines* – the financial press often carries features on mutual funds, and a manager with an alert public relations officer will take advantage of such opportunities.
- *Promotional mailings* – lists of names and addresses are available from many sources, but the quality is variable. There is considerable debate about the merits of 'blanket' mailing (mailing to as many people as possible, regardless of quality, known on the Internet as 'spamming') compared with 'targeted' mailing. Targeting techniques are now sophisticated, for example using 'socio-demographics' to identify individuals more likely to invest in mutual funds or obtaining a list of applicants for a recent issue of shares.

Another type of targeting concentrates on specific types of institutional investor, such as charities, with a fund specially constructed for their needs and tax status.

Many managers find that their existing investors are a good source of new investment, although they have to guard against promotions that may encourage switching between funds rather than additional investment. The requirement to publish fund reports on a regular basis can be used as a further opportunity to include promotional material with the mailing.

When selecting names for inclusion in a mailing, the manager will take care not to breach any data protection regulations. If a person asks to be excluded from future mailings, that request should be respected.

Many managers do not have adequate facilities to handle the physical aspects of a promotional mailing. They may use a specialist mailing service, therefore, that can provide:

- mailing lists;
- de-duplication (only one envelope per household);
- geographic sorting (to obtain discounts on postage charges);
- personalised printed cover letters;
- 'stuffing' – putting material into envelopes and mailing.

- *Publicity material* – many managers have brochures and leaflets describing their products and providing explanations of particular features. Fund reports, prospectuses, scheme particulars and 'key features documents' are usually prepared to act as promotional literature, as well as to satisfy the regulatory requirements.

- *Trade shows and conferences* – trade shows, often held in conjunction with a conference, can be useful for increasing name awareness amongst institutional investors and intermediaries, by way of exhibiting or by providing a speaker.

- *Sales offices* – some managers of mutual funds have offices in strategic locations around the country (and in some cases, around the world) that may serve merely as a 'home base' for sales staff or consultants, or they can be open to the public and accept direct applications for investment.

Chapter
7

....

ADMINISTRATION

This chapter describes the administrative functions associated with managing a mutual fund, separated under four headings:

* Investment portfolio – maintenance and records of the assets of the fund.
* Valuation, pricing and dealing – dealing in the shares or units of the fund with investors.
* Investors or participants – administration and records for the share- or unit holders, including settlement, maintenance of the register and the allocation of income.
* Communicating with investors – statements, fund reports and accounts tell investors how the fund is progressing. Meetings give investors the opportunity to talk to the fund managers.

7.1 INVESTMENT PORTFOLIO

The investment portfolio comprises the investments held by the mutual fund. Most funds will have between 50 and 100 different holdings, and some will have in excess of 100 holdings. It is essential, therefore, that precise and up-to-date details are maintained and readily available, both of transactions and the resulting portfolio, and of the rights attaching to individual holdings, especially in relation to income, whether dividends or interest.

Purchases and sales

Each time the investment manager buys or sells an investment there are key details to be recorded about the transaction:

- date and time;
- description of the investment, name of company, type of share or stock;
- price paid or received;
- amount, number of shares or amount of stock;
- consideration or proceeds;
- rate and amount of commission and other charges/ duties added or deducted;
- identity of the broker;
- identity of the investment manager.

It is important to record the exact description of the investment, preferably with a reference code as used by the relevant stock exchange, as there are many securities with similar names but considerably different prices and other characteristics.

The broker will normally issue (possibly electronically) a confirmation or contract note confirming the deal and defining the settlement terms (when and how payment should be made). The fund manager will compare this confirmation with the record of the deal, and investigate discrepancies immediately.

Details of the portfolio for each fund are kept in an *investment register*. For each investment there will be entries for an opening balance, each purchase and sale transaction, and the current holding. The average cost of each investment is usually included as well.

The investment register provides:

- opening and current balances of each investment;
- an audit trail of transactions that can be linked to the original deals;
- the costs of purchases and proceeds of sales.

For example:

The XYZ fund

ABC Inc.

	Opening balance			30,000
30/01/99	Purchase	@$1.00	10,000	
28/02/01	Purchase	@$1.35	5,000	
01/04/03	Sale	@$1.54	−17,250	
	Current balance			27,750

DEF Inc.

	Opening balance			0
30/03/99	Purchase	@$2.50	25,000	
27/04/02	Purchase	@$2.35	35,000	
	Current balance			60,000

The investment manager may place one deal on behalf of two or more funds, and may obtain a lower rate of commission because of the increased size of the transaction. As far as the investment register is concerned, however, a separate record is needed for each fund and the entries for each holding will be determined by the manager's allocation policy for aggregated or bulked transactions.

From this information, profits and losses on sales can be computed, valuations determined and entitlements to rights, including dividends or interest, confirmed. Periodically the records are reconciled with those held by the custodian or trustee.

Settlement

Settlement, like dealing, may be achieved electronically. The terms of settlement are included in brokers' confirmations. The custodian, depositary or trustee is responsible for ensuring conformity with the terms, but will double-check that the fund has sufficient liquidity to pay for purchases, or stock to support sales. Unless borrowing is permitted (if it is, it is usually only for a very short term and against expected receipts), the custodian may delay settlement of purchases until the manager generates sufficient cash.

Custody

The custodian, depositary or trustee is responsible for:

- registering the fund's legal title to shares or other securities;
- the safekeeping of share certificates and similar documentation;

- ensuring that the entry on the underlying register is correct.

Accounting

The fund manager maintains accounting records for each mutual fund it operates, from which a set of accounts can be produced. The records must be maintained according to rules and standards stipulated by local regulations. Accounting conventions vary from country to country, defined by, for example, Statements of Recommended Practice.

In general, each fund has a capital account and an income account. If there is sufficient income there will also be a distribution account. Each fund has an annual accounting date and stated accounting periods (two each year is typical, although monthly accounting periods are growing in popularity), which govern the timing of publication of fund reports and accounts.

On the last day of the period, the accounts are 'frozen', with totals carried forward or transferred to the next period. This allows the accounts for one period to be finalised whilst activity in the next continues to be recorded.

The *capital account* may include:

- the value of the property of the fund at the start of the period;

- the amount of cash received on the issue or creation of new shares or units;
- the amount of cash paid out on the redemption or cancellation of shares or units repurchased from outgoing investors;
- the net increase or decrease in the value of the property of the fund over the period;
- a statement of net realised profits or losses during the period;
- the amount of realised net capital gains paid out if allowed to be distributed;
- any charges and expenses charged to capital;
- information about dealing commission incurred;
- the value of the property of the fund at the end of the period.

The *income account* may include:

- the total income from the assets of the scheme (dividends, interest);
- the total of any other income, e.g. underwriting fees;
- charges paid to the manager for its services;
- fees or expenses paid to the custodian, depositary or trustee;
- the auditor's fees;
- total amount of tax deducted before distribution to holders;
- any balance brought forward from the last period;
- the amount of any interim allocation of net income;
- the amount of final allocation of net income;
- any balance carried forward to the next period.

If the fund is a trust, substantially all the income must be allocated to holders at the end of the annual accounting period. A similar requirement applies if the fund is not to account for tax on income, as in the US for example.

The *distribution account* records the total income to be allocated to holders. The amount at any time depends on whether the current distribution is an interim distribution or the final distribution for the accounting year. The actual amount per share or unit is determined by the manager and agreed with the trustee or depositary and arrangements made for it to be:

- paid to holders who require income, or
- reinvested in the fund, either to purchase additional units or shares or for the benefit of holders of accumulation units or shares.

The totals in the distribution account will be reconciled with the sum of the individual holders' allocations. Most jurisdictions will allow managers to retain and carry forward very small amounts of income that are uneconomic to distribute but this apart the income account should finish the accounting year with a zero balance after transfers to the distribution account.

Income collection

The fund's custodian, depositary or trustee, as the registered legal owner, is normally responsible for income collection, including foreign tax reclaims.

A mutual fund's income comprises dividends from equity investments, interest from stocks, bonds and bank deposits and other items such as underwriting fees. Since the investment manager is likely to have an income target for each accounting period, he or she will want routine confirmation that that rate of distribution can be maintained or increased. Investment administration staff will prepare income forecasts for the period, particularly on dividends (amounts and payment dates). Some adjustments will be made when the actual details are available, and the portfolio manager may have to make some changes to the investments to achieve the fund's target.

An essential check is that expected income is received, and that any missing items or discrepancies are investigated. This may be more difficult for overseas investments, especially those traded on emerging or less developed markets.

7.2 VALUATION, PRICING AND DEALING

Valuation

The value of a mutual fund depends on the prices or values of the underlying securities and other assets held by the fund. The manager must carry out regular valuations of the fund's property, so that the prices at which shares or units may be bought and sold can be calculated. Regulations usually prescribe how often valuations must be performed. In the UK, for example, the required minimum frequency is twice each month. The majority of funds are valued on a daily basis, but some managers prefer a weekly valuation, and some carry out more than one each day.

In most countries, the manager is required to perform a single valuation, based on the mid-market prices for the securities held by the fund. In the UK, however, a *dual pricing system* is still permitted for unit trusts, requiring two separate valuations, one using offer prices and the other using bid prices. Although initially UK OEICs had to be single-priced the flexibility to dual-price applies from February 2007.

Regulators normally require the prospectus or scheme particulars of a mutual fund to specify the days and the time of day that a valuation will be carried out, sometimes known as the *valuation point*, and to set out the manager's policy for valuing each type of asset held in the fund. This policy may be no more than is prescribed in regulations but the overall requirement is for it to be fair and consistently applied.

Pricing

Once the valuation of the fund's property is complete the share or unit prices can be calculated. Although shares or units generally are traded at a single price, regulations may require several prices to be calculated. For example, the UK unit trust dual pricing model requires:

- the price the manager will pay to the trustee to create new units – the *creation price*;
- the price the manager will receive when units are cancelled – the *cancellation price*;
- the price an investor will pay when buying units – the *buying or offer price*;
- the price an investor will receive when selling units back to the manager – the *bid or selling price.*

Exact details differ between countries, but regulations specify the calculations required, how maximum and minimum prices are determined, and the accuracy to which they are expressed. An example valuation and price calculation follows:

The XYZ Fund – 1,000,000 shares/units in issue

Investments	Shares held	Price	Value
Company A	100,000	2.500	250,000
Company B	500,000	10.162	5,081,000
Company C	200,000	8.210	1,642,000
Total value of investments			6,973,000
Cash			**327,000**
Total capital value			7,300,000
Net income			
Accrued income, less expenses and taxation			512,345
Total net asset value (NAV)			**7,812,345**

Share/unit price
(7,812,345 divided by 1,000,000 shares/units in issue)

– unrounded	7.812345
– adjusted to 4 significant figures	7.812

Dealing

Shares or units in a mutual fund have to be created before they can be issued. Once created, the shares or units are issued by the manager to any individual or company who applies to buy them, at the NAV price plus any front-end charges to give the asked or buying price, unless the charges are to be shown separately. The manager must disclose whether dealing prices are 'historic' or 'forward'. Historic pricing means the investor's transaction will receive the last calculated price, whereas forward pricing means the investor will receive the next calculated price.

Managers often hold a supply (in the UK, the 'box') of shares or units so that they can act as market makers, buying and selling shares or units from and to investors without changing the total number in issue. In some countries, regulations require that the manager must not go short of shares or units; each day enough shares or units must be created to satisfy all trades contracted by the manager.

The shares or units may be listed on an exchange, in which case they can be bought and sold like any other security. If a listing is obtained, regulators are keen to ensure that prices quoted do not vary significantly from the manager's net asset value (NAV)-based price. If a share- or unit holder wishes to sell the holding, the manager will redeem the shares or units at the bid or selling price, which is the NAV price calculated from market dealing bid prices, after adjusting for dealing charges.

A withdrawal fee or redemption charge may be imposed, although this would usually be instead of an initial charge, and is often on a sliding scale, as described in Section 4.6.

If more holders are selling shares or units back to the manager than there are purchasers, and the manager does not wish to hold them, they can be cancelled. The shares or units then cease to exist.

7.3 INVESTORS/PARTICIPANTS

Buying and selling

Although some funds are exchange-traded, the shares or units of most mutual funds are bought and sold by making an application to the manager. This can be in writing, by telephone or via the Internet, directly by the investor or by the investor's adviser or agent. Many managers have pre-printed application and redemption forms and their advertisements and other promotional mailing material often include an application form. Once accepted by the manager, applications constitute a binding contract, and the manager issues a *contract note* stating the details of the transaction.

For purchases, payment can be included with the application. Some managers may insist on this for the initial investment of a first-time investor. Alternatively, the contract note will specify when payment is required. For large investments, the manager may be required by law to obtain confirmation of the investor's identification and of the source or destination of money involved in the transaction: if there is any suspicion that the money is being laundered, or used to support terrorist activity, the suspicion must be reported to the authorities.

If the order to purchase shares or units has been made through an intermediary, the investor might have a right to change his or her mind and cancel the transaction. This often applies when the investor has received advice or the transaction is not completed via face-to-face meetings at which fund documents can be supplied. In these cases, a notice of *cancellation rights* is sent direct to the investor, who typically is then allowed 14 days to exercise the right to cancel. With this as a protection, the EU's *Distance Marketing Directive,* which seeks to outlaw other than face-to-face dealing, can be relaxed in cases where approved intermediaries place orders on behalf of their clients over the telephone or by electronic means.

For sales or redemptions, the holder may have to complete a form of redemption or renunciation, renouncing their interest in the shares or units being sold. The manager will not pay the proceeds until the form has been completed and returned. Client money regulations may be in place and require that proceeds be paid to the registered first-named holder, unless written and signed instructions have been received directing otherwise. Intermediaries, if authorised to handle their clients' money, may receive proceeds from the manager but must hold it in a separate client money (bank) account.

Registration

A register of share- or unit holders must be maintained, and usually by the manager or an appointed registrar or transfer agent. In the case of a trust, responsibility sometimes lies with the trustee but for a company, it is usually performed by the company itself or delegated, either to the manager or to a specialist third party known as the registrar or transfer agent.

The entry on the register is the conclusive evidence of an investor's title to the shares or units. Details recorded should include:

• the name and address of the holder;
• the number of shares or units of each type held by each holder;
• the date on which the holder was registered.

Because the information held on the register is deemed to comprise the conclusive legal record of ownership, it must be accurate, complete and up to date. The register must also be available for inspection by the holders, for confirmation purposes, free of charge, during normal business hours, but may not necessarily be available to the general public.

As well as establishing and maintaining the register, the registrar or transfer agent is responsible for:

• ensuring that the number of shares or units recorded on the register reconciles with the total number of shares or units in issue;

- issuing certificates if there is a requirement for them;
- allocating net income to share- or unit holders;
- preparing and dispatching payments representing the distribution of income, which may include realised capital gains.

There are several types of transaction that the registrar will process:

Issues and redemptions – the registrar will register a holding once the manager confirms that payment and full registration details have been received and pay out the proceeds on redemption once written confirmation or renounced certificates have been received.

Transfers – shares or units in a mutual fund are transferable securities, and can be transferred from one holder to another, usually by completion of a stock transfer form, sent to the registrar with payment of any appropriate transfer tax or stamp duty.

'Operation of law' – this refers to the transmission of title to a holding upon the death or bankruptcy of a holder (or liquidation in the case of corporate holders). In the case of a joint holding, if one of the joint holders dies, the surviving holders are recognised as having title to the shares or units, subject to any contradictory information concerning the nature of the joint holding arrangement. The registrar will need to see the death certificate. In the case of a sole holding, authority to deal

with the holding rests with the executors or administrators of the deceased holder's estate. They must supply the registrar with evidence both of death and of their authority to act but can then arrange with the registrar for either the transfer of shares or units to themselves or to the beneficiaries, or the sale of the holding.

Conversions – this may refer to reinvestment from one mutual fund to another run by the same manager (also called 'switching'), or to a change in type of share or unit held in a single fund.

Change of name or address – the registrar needs to be sure that the source of the instruction to make the change is proper, such as a written confirmation signed by the holder recorded on the register.

Enquiries and requests for information – to avoid breaching data protection regulations, specific details should be sent by mail only to the registered holder at the registered address, unless the manager or registrar is certain of the identity of the person making the enquiry.

Some jurisdictions allow the issue of bearer shares, and in this case no register is maintained. Holders receive coupons at the time of their original investment and, when income distributions are to be made, the bearer must present the relevant coupon to a paying agent to receive the entitlement. Coupons must be passed on to any subsequent purchaser.

Income allocations

After the net income (including if permitted net realised capital gains) per share or unit has been calculated, it is allocated to share- or unit holders in proportion to their holding. The tax authorities may require that allocations and distributions are processed net of tax, in which case *tax credit vouchers* are sent to the holders, stating how much tax has been paid on their behalf.

The registrar checks that the sum of all the individual payments of income being distributed and the amounts being retained or reinvested on behalf of holders is the same as the total amount allocated. This requires an equitable method of rounding payments to the nearest unit of currency.

Payment is made by one of the following methods:

- warrant (a guaranteed cheque), payable to the first-named holder, and sent to the address held on the register;
- warrant payable to a third party, if there are written instructions to this effect signed by the holder(s);
- direct credit to a bank or similar account, using a facility such as in the UK – the Bankers Automated Clearing System (BACS).

There are several advantages of using an automatic crediting facility. For the holder these include:

- no risk of the warrant being lost or delayed in the post;

- the payment is credited on the due date, with no clearing delay;
- the holder does not need to visit the bank to pay in the warrant.

For the registrar/transfer or paying agent:

- minimal paper handling;
- fewer reconciliation problems;
- reduced costs.

Warrants are only valid for a limited period, usually six months, and any not presented within this time will have to be returned to the paying agent for re-dating. If the payment remains unclaimed for a long time (typically six years but sometimes 12 years), it is transferred back into the capital property of the fund, and is not reclaimable.

7.4 COMMUNICATING WITH INVESTORS

Transaction confirmations

Regulators normally require managers to issue investors with transaction confirmations or contract notes within 24 hours of the transaction being executed, specifying details of the transaction, including the date and time of execution, fund name, quantity and type of share/unit, price, consideration or proceeds and of any charges added or deducted.

Statements

At periodic intervals specified by regulators or when payments are made to holders, or income is reinvested, a *statement* is sent to each holder showing:

- the number of shares or units currently held;
- the payment date and rate per share or unit;
- the amount of the payment;
- the amount of any tax credit.

A valuation of the holding and a list of transactions since the last statement may be included.

Accounts

The *accounts* of a mutual fund are usually included in the fund report. They are drawn up in accordance with the country's regulations and accounting practice. The accounts provide:

- a statement of assets and liabilities;
- details of the capital account;
- details of the income and distribution accounts;
- notes describing the accounting policies used and giving explanations of certain items.

Fund reports

The manager is responsible for preparing the *fund report*, which is sent to share- or unit holders free of charge, and which must be available for inspection. It is also a useful guide for prospective investors.

The minimum content, frequency and latest publication dates are prescribed by regulations. In most countries annual and half-yearly or *interim* reports are mandatory, although it may be permissible to exclude some matters from the interim report. The manager must issue the report within a reasonable time from the end of the accounting period, e.g. eight weeks. Most managers find it convenient to send the report out with the income allocation statement, warrant and tax credit voucher (as appropriate).

Typically, a fund's annual report contains:

- the names and addresses of the manager, custodian, depositary or trustee, registrar, auditor, investment adviser;
- the fund's investment objectives;
- a review of the manager's investment activities during the reporting period;
- a description of any significant change in the prospectus or scheme particulars since the last report;
- the value of the property of the fund at the beginning and end of the reporting period;
- the portfolio statement;
- details of changes to the investments since the last report;
- the cost of purchases of investments;
- the proceeds of sales of investments;

- a comparative table detailing the performance record for the fund since it was launched, or for a shorter period if permitted, in terms of:
  ○ the highest and lowest prices each year
  ○ the net asset value of the property at the end of each year
  ○ the number of shares or units in existence;
- the trustee's or depositary's report confirming (or otherwise) that the manager has managed the fund during the period in accordance with the regulations and investment objectives;
- the auditor's report confirming (or otherwise) that the accounts have been properly prepared, and give a true and fair view of the financial position of the fund at the end of the period and of the net income for the period;
- accounts or financial statements.

Meetings – AGMs and EGMs

Mutual funds constituted as investment companies may be required to hold an *annual general meeting (AGM)* of shareholders, but those constituted as trusts do not. In either case, circumstances will arise that require there to be *extraordinary general meetings (EGMs)* for holders to agree to:

- any significant or material change to the fund's constitution;
- the fund's winding-up;
- amalgamate or merge the fund with another fund;

- any material departure from the investment objectives of the fund;
- removal of the manager.

Share- or unit holders must be given adequate notice of the meeting (usually 14 days), and the notice must set out the place, day and time of the meeting, and the terms of any resolutions to be proposed.

The meeting cannot proceed unless a quorum of share- or unit holders is present. The *quorum* comprises holders present in person or by proxy, representing a specified minimum number or proportion of holders or of the value of the shares or units in issue at the relevant time. If a quorum is not present within, say, 30 minutes after the appointed time, the meeting is adjourned, but at an adjourned meeting the holders present may constitute a quorum, whatever their number.

Each resolution must be voted on separately. This may be by *show of hands*, or, if demanded, by a *poll*. A vote by poll allows one vote for each share or unit held, and is always demanded for material changes.

The manager, though entitled to receive notice of and attend meetings of holders, is not normally entitled to vote or be counted in the quorum.

Voting by proxy

Holders who would like to vote at a meeting, but are unable to attend, can use or send a *proxy* to vote on their behalf. A special form of proxy usually is sent to holders with the notice of meeting so that they may cast their votes in advance. Proxy forms must be returned within a specified time before the meeting, normally 48 hours.

In effect, the holder appoints someone (usually the chairperson of the meeting) as his or her proxy, to cast the votes for or against each resolution as specified on the proxy form. Alternatively, the holder may simply appoint a proxy to attend and vote on his or her behalf as the proxy sees fit. Should the holder decide to attend after all, he or she may, but is not obliged to, revoke the proxy and cast his or her votes personally.

A resolution is passed if a specified majority of votes cast are cast in favour. Ordinary resolutions require only a simple majority, i.e. 50% plus 1; extraordinary or special resolutions usually require a higher percentage, which in the UK must be at least 75%; in the US, it is 67% provided at least 50% of the total possible votes are represented at the meeting.

Minutes of meetings must be made, recording all proceedings and resolutions passed, including the results of voting. Minutes are usually the responsibility of the manager.

Chapter

8

....

TAXATION

This chapter describes the typical taxation treatment of a mutual fund and the taxation implications for individual participants or investors as share- or unit holders.

8.1 INTRODUCTION

The general aim of taxation laws is to produce the same outcome in relation to the tax position of an investor in mutual funds as would arise from direct investment. Investment via a mutual fund should not give rise to any double taxation of income or gains. Any tax that is withheld or deducted from proceeds of sale, or from distributions that would not ordinarily be due from the recipient on a direct investment, can either be recovered from the relevant tax authority, or offset against any associated liability.

This applies equally to investment by residents and non-residents of the mutual fund's home state or country. To facilitate cross-border investment, most Governments have entered into *double taxation agreements* with each other, whereby tax suffered in one country is recoverable or capable of offset by a resident of another country. Some countries go further to encourage investment in local funds by agreeing to pay distributions to non-residents free of any tax. France, Germany, Luxembourg and the US, for example, allow mutual funds to choose to be treated as a conduit for most tax purposes, and not pay taxes themselves on net income and capital gains that are distributed to shareholders or reinvested for them. The individuals are then liable to account to the authorities for any tax that is due.

Governments may also introduce specific tax incentives for individuals to build up investment funds, either in order to broaden the country's investor base, or to encourage individuals to provide for their own welfare, particularly provision for health care and retirement pensions.

Examples are the 401(k) and IRAs (Individual Retirement Accounts) operated in the US, Personal Equity Plans (PEPs – up to 5 April 1999), then Individual Savings Accounts (ISAs) in the UK and the Pooled Retirement Funds in Hong Kong. Contributions to such plans are either tax deductible at the time of contribution or the benefits accrue within them free of tax. Any tax liability is accordingly deferred until investment in the fund is realised or withdrawals are made, although even at this stage there may be relief from normal taxation.

The more liberal the treatment of non-residents for tax purposes, the more likely is their evasion of tax liability in their home state or country. The EU recently introduced a 'Savings Directive', described as a measure to combat tax avoidance, by requiring the paying agents in each Member State to provide details of interest payments made to non-residents to their national authority, who must share this information with the non-resident investors' home state authorities so that they may collect tax from individual investors. These requirements have prompted some countries who previously paid income gross to non-residents to now pay them under deduction of a withholding tax.

8.2 THE FUND

The policy of most jurisdictions is to treat the mutual fund as a company subject to corporate or income tax only on its ordinary business (i.e. net income arising from holding investments), and exempt it from taxation on its gains from buying and selling investments. In the US, provided the gains and net income are distributed, the fund does not pay federal income tax on either. Taxes are the responsibility of and paid by the shareholders under a *'pass-through'* arrangement, whether they choose to receive cash or reinvest their entitlement.

In most other countries, distributions of capital are not permitted, except on a winding-up. If capital gains are subject to taxation, it is collected from the share and unit holders if they realise a gain when they sell their investment in the fund.

The fund may suffer other taxes in various forms in its investment and its administrative activities, both directly and indirectly. Examples are:

- sales taxes or value added taxes on the buying of goods and services used in the administrative management of the fund;
- duties payable when buying or selling securities; and
- taxation deducted or withheld from receipts of income on investments, to the extent they are not recoverable or offset against the fund's liability to tax.

It is usual for the fund's activities to be distinguished according to whether they are concerned with:

- capital – the investment portfolio (including uninvested cash) created from contributors' capital investment, or
- income or net income – the income arising from the investments less the expenses of management.

Together they comprise the fund's net asset value (NAV).

Capital

Mutual funds are normally exempted from any tax on the results of portfolio transactions, but may suffer taxes or duties applicable to the transactions themselves, in the same way as any other investor or trader in securities, e.g. contract or transfer duty. Such taxes are included in the consideration for buying securities or deducted from the proceeds of sale.

Otherwise, net capital gains from managing the portfolio of investments usually accrue within the fund entirely tax-free, provided the rate at which the fund manager makes investment changes is not excessive. Most tax authorities reserve the right to revoke a fund's special status for tax purposes if it is adjudged that trading, rather than investment, is its purpose.

Some jurisdictions allow certain expenses of management to be deducted in whole or in part from the fund's capital.

If this is permitted, the ability to deduct the expense from the income for tax purposes may be restricted, or else the net-of-tax value of the expense only may be taken from capital.

Income

Whether and how the net income of a fund is taxed is a function of the cash flow needs of the Government of the home country, and its attitude towards its citizens as being good at declaring their taxable income. Income should be taxed only once, either in the hands of the fund or in the hands of its ultimate beneficiaries, the share- or unit holders.

Most jurisdictions collect tax from the fund. Even the US will tax the fund if it does not satisfy the requirements for *pass-through*.

The basis for any tax charge reflects any tax actually (or deemed to have been) deducted, withheld or otherwise accounted for by the paying entity. For example, dividends received from companies will have been paid out of the companies' net income after tax. Receipts of such income by mutual funds should not be subject to any further tax. Similarly, the local tax to which foreign income is subject may be reduced by the amount of any foreign tax withheld.

The general computation is as follows:

1. Gross income that has not already been fully taxed, *less*
2. Expenses of management and amortisation of capital costs allowable as deductions for tax purposes, *equals*
3. Net income subject to taxation.

The actual taxation to be paid will be reduced by credit for foreign taxes withheld (but typically not the foreign corporation tax suffered by the paying company) where double tax agreements exist, or by an expense deduction.

Local tax rules specify which management expenses are deductible for tax purposes, and how capital expenses, such as costs of formation or of the furniture and equipment that may be part of the fund's assets, may be amortised against net income. Normally, the tax treatment follows the accounting treatment specified within the principal regulations, but this is not always so.

Other

The other taxes that may be suffered by a mutual fund or its operator include:

• a sales or value added tax (VAT) which is added to fees or commissions charged by brokers, sales agents, custodians, transfer agents, investment managers, administrators; and

- duties payable on the purchase or sale of securities (e.g. stamp duty on the purchase of UK equities by UK residents).

Whether or not the fund can treat such taxes or duties as credits or charges depends on local tax rules.

8.3 THE INVESTOR/PARTICIPANT

The descriptions following are those generally applicable to investors who are residents of the country in which the fund is established. The treatment of non-residents will almost certainly be different and subject to various concessions, such as receiving distributions without deduction of tax.

Capital gains and losses

Normally, investors are not subject to taxation on unrealised gains, but to taxation on realised gains (less losses) on their sale of a mutual fund's shares or units, exactly as they are on the sale of any other investment. This may mean a separately collected capital gains tax, or simply an additional amount of income subject to income tax.

The amount of taxable gain is computed as the difference between sale proceeds and purchase cost. If either the total holding is not disposed of, or if the amount sold was not all acquired at the same time or cost, then some form of averaging or apportionment is necessary to establish the amount of gain.

Other adjustments may be required, depending upon local rules. In the UK, for example, the base cost of purchase may be inflated by a factor representing the rise in the general index used to measure purchasing power or inflation (the *retail prices index*). Conversely, it may be necessary to reduce the base cost of purchase by the portion of the first distribution after purchase, which represents a return of the income included in the buying price. Such an amount (known in the UK as equalisation) is not taxable as income, but is treated as a return of part of the capital investment.

Income distributions

If income is taxed at source (i.e. accounted for by the mutual fund), the participants receive, along with the net amount, a certificate of taxation already paid or accounted for by the fund. The tax represented by this certificate serves either to discharge the participants' personal liability, or as a credit against their liability at higher rates. Depending on local rules, if the participant is not subject to taxation, the certificate may be used to support a claim for a tax refund from the authorities, subject to any restrictions over such claims.

Recipients who themselves are corporations may be able either to avoid any further taxation on income received from mutual funds, or to treat the tax withheld or deducted as a credit against their liability to corporate taxes.

Special rules may apply to income distributed to non-residents. For example, rather than withholding local taxes, the distribution is paid gross (i.e. without deduction of any tax). Similar concessions may be available to holders who are not liable to taxation, which might include charities or pension funds.

If income is distributed without any withholding or deduction of taxes, recipients will be liable to account to the local tax authorities for any tax that is due on the amount of the distribution, at the rates applicable to their status as taxpayers. The requirements of the EU's Savings Directive regarding interest payments to non-residents have already been mentioned in this respect.

Different rules may apply as between bond funds and equity funds, depending on whether the local jurisdiction treats distributions of bond interest differently from distributions of equity dividends.

GLOSSARY OF INDUSTRY TERMS

· ·

NOTE: includes terms in common use, not all of which are necessarily found in the text.

Accumulation   Adding income to capital instead of distributing it as dividend.

Accumulation units   Net income is automatically retained in the fund and reflected in the unit price.

Active management   An investment management approach that seeks to outperform the market through the application of informed, independent judgement. The opposite of passive management.

Administrator   An organisation that provides administrative services to a fund or its management company or trustee.

Adviser   The individual or organisation employed by a mutual fund to direct the investment and management of the fund's assets.

Annual charge   A charge levied for the management of the mutual fund.

Annual report   A yearly statement of the financial progress and status of a mutual fund.

Asked price (US)   Price based on the net asset value (NAV) plus sales charge, paid when purchasing shares (see *Offer price*).

Asset allocation   The method by which the investment manager determines the spread and mix of securities and assets in which the fund's capital is invested.

Authorised unit trust (UK)   A unit trust scheme authorised by the Financial Services Authority.

Automatic reinvestment   The use of income or realised capital gains for the purchase of additional shares or units of a mutual fund.

Back end load   A charge levied when units are redeemed.

Balanced fund   A fund with a portfolio comprising a mix of bonds and equities.

Basis point (BP)   The smallest unit of yield or interest rate measurement equal to 0.01 %.

Bear   Someone who thinks a market or price will fall.

Bear market   A market where prices are influenced by sellers.

Benchmark   A notional or actual comparator for performance, such as an index.

Bid basis   Mutual fund prices are based on bid prices.

Bid/offer spread   The difference between the bid and offer prices expressed either as an amount or as a % of the offer price.

Bid price   The price paid to holders redeeming their holdings.

Blue chip   Shares in companies which are highly regarded, usually large and well established.

Bond   A marketable debt instrument issued by a company or government.

Bond fund   A mutual fund with a portfolio that consists primarily of bonds.

Book or box   Stock of shares or units held by managers as principals.

Bull   Someone who thinks a market or price will rise.

Bull market   A market where prices are influenced by buyers; i.e. prices are rising.

Cancellation price (UK)   The price payable to the manager by the trustee for units cancelled and the lowest price at which managers may repurchase units, based on the bid prices of underlying investments.

Cancellation rights   In certain circumstances an investor has the right to cancel a purchase of shares or units.

Capital gains distribution   Payments to mutual fund holders of their proportionate interests in realised gains from the sales of securities in the fund's underlying portfolio.

Capital gains tax (CGT)   Tax payable on gains arising from the sale of securities.

Cash equivalent Short-term bonds, notes and repurchase agreements, usually government backed.

Closed-ended fund A fund with a fixed amount of capital issuing a limited number of shares.

Collateral Security pledged as guarantee of repayment.

Collective investment scheme Generic name for pooled, investment or mutual funds.

Commission A fee paid by the manager to a third party agent or intermediary for introducing business.

Contract note Document sent to the investor when a purchase or sale is made, with details of the transaction.

Conversion factor (UK) The factor linking accumulation and income units.

Conversion of units (UK) Changing an investment from accumulation to income units, or vice versa.

Cost averaging For regular savings the average price per share or unit paid by the holder can be lower than the average price for the period in which savings are made.

Cum distribution Includes the income distribution. The buyer is entitled to the next distribution.

Custodian A bank or trust company that takes custody of mutual fund assets and securities for safekeeping.

Debenture Bond of company acknowledging debt and providing for payment of interest at fixed intervals.

Dematerialisation The process of ceasing to issue certificates to investors.

Depositary An institution which acts as custodian of assets on behalf of shareholders.

Derivatives Securities whose values are linked to, or derived from, other securities.

Distributions Payments of investment income or realised capital gains to mutual fund share- or unit holders.

Diversification Spreading investments and risk among a number of securities across geographic, economic and industrial sectors and asset classes.

Earnings The profit available for equity holders.

Eligible market A securities market in which a mutual fund can invest.

Equity shares Shares in a company that are entitled to the balance of profits and assets after all prior charges.

Equities fund A mutual fund that invests primarily in equity shares.

Ex-distribution (XD) Excludes the income distribution. The seller is entitled to the next distribution.

Ex-distribution price (XD price) A price that excludes entitlement to the next income distribution.

Exempt funds Mutual funds for tax-exempt bodies.

Exit charge Charge levied on redemption of shares or units (see also *Back end load*).

Feeder fund (UK) A relevant pension scheme dedicated to a single collective investment scheme.

Fiduciary Individual given the legal power to participate in the management of assets for the benefit of others.

Forward pricing Investors deal at the unit prices determined at the next valuation point.

Franked income (UK) Dividends received from UK companies after payment of UK corporation tax.

Front end load A sales charge levied on the purchase of units.

FSA (UK) Financial Services Authority.

Fund of funds A mutual fund that may only invest in other mutual funds.

Futures and options fund (FOF) A mutual fund that invests in approved and other derivatives (where most or all the transactions are fully covered by cash, securities or other derivatives).

Geared futures and options fund (GFOF) A mutual fund that is allowed to borrow and invests in approved and other derivatives (where most or all the investment is limited by the amount of property available).

Gearing Increasing the funds available for investment by borrowing (see also *Leveraging*).

Hedging The process of protecting a fund's assets from the effects of exposure to currency fluctuations or other investment risks.

Hedge fund A fund that uses a variety of techniques, including long/short positioning, and strategies utilising derivative instruments with the aim of making profits in rising and falling markets; also known as 'alternative investment strategies' or 'absolute return' funds.

Historic pricing Investors deal at the unit prices determined at the most recent valuation point.

Hybrid fund Same as 'Balanced fund'.

IFA Independent financial adviser.

Incentive compensation A fee paid to the investment adviser determined by fund performance in relation to specified market indices.

Income fund A mutual fund whose objective is to provide income on a regular basis.

Income units Units where income is paid to unit holders.

Index fund A mutual fund that aims to match the performance of a particular index; either comprises the securities making up the index being followed or models the index by a combination of major holdings and derivatives; also known as 'Tracker funds'.

Initial charge Charge levied on investors when units or shares are purchased (see *Front end load*).

Individual Savings Account (ISA) (UK) A savings plan with tax benefits which replaced PEPs on 6 April 1999.

Initial offer price The price at which units or shares in a new fund are available to the public during the period of offer.

Initial yield An estimated figure that indicates how much income a new mutual fund might expect to receive in the first year.

Interim accounting period The period within the annual accounting period during which income earned by a mutual fund is accumulated before payment to holders.

International fund A mutual fund that invests in securities traded in several different overseas markets.

Investment trust A closed-ended company whose business is to hold and manage a portfolio of investments.

Leveraging Same as 'Gearing'.

Liquidity Part of the mutual fund's portfolio held in cash.

Load (US) A sales charge included in the purchase price.

Manager's box See *Book or box*.

Market capitalisation Total value of a company's issued securities at current market prices.

Management fee The amount paid to mutual fund managers for their services.

Mixed fund Same as 'Balanced fund'.

Money market fund A mutual fund that invests in deposits and other money market instruments.

Mutual fund An open-ended investment company or trust which combines the contributions of many investors with similar objectives.

NASD (US) National Association of Securities Dealers.

NASDAQ (US) National Association of Securities Dealers Automated Quotations: a system that gathers, stores and displays quotations of trading prices.

Net assets The total assets of a mutual fund less current liabilities.

Net asset value (NAV) The value of the underlying shares held based on quoted mid-market prices and other assets, less liabilities, divided by the number of shares in issue.

No-load fund A mutual fund with no front-end sales charge.

Nominal value The face value of a share.

Nominee A legal entity that holds shares on behalf of another entity.

Non-certificated Shares or units for which no certificate is issued.

Offer basis Mutual fund prices are based on offer prices.

Offer price The price paid by investors when buying shares or units.

Off-the-page advertisements Advertisements that appear in the press and contain an application form.

Open-ended fund A fund with variable capital allowed to issue or to redeem units on a continuous basis.

Par value See *Nominal value.*

Passive management Portfolio management decisions are taken only when pre-specified changes occur in an external reference, such as the composition of an index.

Periodic charge See *Annual charge.*

Performance fee Additional fee charged by managers based on performance of the fund; common practice in hedge fund management.

Personal Equity Plan (PEP) (UK) An investment plan that is free of tax on any income or capital gain.

Portfolio The securities owned by a mutual fund.

Preliminary charge See *Initial charge.*

Product particulars Factual information about the investment.

Prospectus   The official publication that describes the objectives, policies, services, management, restrictions and charges, etc., of a mutual fund.

Purchase price   See *Offer price*.

Redemption price   See *Bid price*.

Registrar   The company that maintains the register of holders.

Regular income plan   Uses several mutual funds to provide monthly or quarterly income.

Renunciation form   The formal transfer to the manager of shares or units being redeemed.

Rights issue   An issue of new shares to existing shareholders in a fixed proportion to their holdings.

Sales charge   A front-end charge included in the purchase price of a mutual fund.

Savings plan   Scheme run by mutual fund managers whereby investors purchase units on a regular basis.

Scheme particulars (UK)   A document that provides full details of the fund and how it operates.

Scrip issue   An issue of shares to existing shareholders in set proportion to their holdings in lieu of monetary dividend.

Securities Exchange Commission (SEC) (US)   The federal agency that promotes full public disclosure and protects the investing public against malpractice in securities markets.

Securities & Investment Institute (UK)   The professional body for qualified and experienced practitioners of good repute engaged in securities and other financial services.

Share exchange scheme   A scheme that enables investors to exchange equity holdings for shares or units in a mutual fund.

SICAF   Société d'Investissement à Capital Fixé – a closed-ended fund of the corporate type frequently used in France and Luxembourg.

SICAV   Société d'Investissement à Capital Variable – an open-ended fund of the corporate type frequently used in France and Luxembourg.

Single pricing   Pricing system where only one price is quoted, rather than separate buying and selling prices.

Standard deviation   Mathematically derived measure of the volatility of returns or prices about their own average.

Stock fund   Same as 'Equities fund'.

Sub-division of shares or units   Shares or units are 'split' in a fixed ratio.

Switching discount   Discount given when an investor switches from one mutual fund to another.

Tax credit voucher   Tax on income, whether distributed or reinvested, is paid automatically to the taxation authority and holders receive a 'voucher' in confirmation.

Total return   A measure of performance that combines income and capital gain or loss.

Tracker fund   See *Index fund*.

Transfer agent (US)   The organisation used by a mutual fund to maintain security records and handle share- or unit holder transactions.

Trust deed   Legal document that contains basic details of the constitution of a mutual fund that is a trust.

Trustee   An institution which acts as custodian of a unit trust's assets on behalf of unit holders.

Umbrella fund   A single authorised fund with any number of constituent parts or sub-funds.

Underwriting   Undertaking to support an issue of shares.

Unfranked income (UK)   Income on which UK corporation tax has not been paid, including interest, fees and dividends from non-UK companies.

UCITS (EU)   Undertakings for Collective Investment in Transferable Securities. A European Directive and a generic label for qualifying EU funds.

Unit trust   A contractual-type fund that operates under trust law, common in the UK and Ireland.

Withholding tax (WHT)   Tax deducted from dividends paid by foreign companies to non-residents.

Yield   The percentage of the quoted offer price that represents the prospective annual income of the mutual fund for its current annual accounting period, after deducting all charges.

Yield to maturity   The effective annual rate of return on a bond including interest and return of capital if held to maturity.

USEFUL CONTACTS

. . . .

	Trade body	Regulators
EUROPE	EFAMA European Fund & Asset Management Association www.efama.org	*See individual countries*
France	AFG – ASFFI Association Francaise de la Gestion Financiere www.afg-asso.fr	Ministry of the Economy and Finance Autorite des Marches Financiers www.amf-france.org
Germany	BVI Bundesverband Deutscher Investment-und- Vermogensverwaltungs- Gesellschaften www.bvi.de	Federal Ministry of Finance Federal Financial Supervisory Authority www.bafin.de
Ireland	DFIA Dublin Funds Industry Assocn www.dfia.ie	Minister for Finance Central Bank and Financial Services Authority of Ireland Irish Financial Services Regulatory Authority www.ifsra.ie
Italy	ASSOGESTIONI Associazione del Risparmio Gestito www.assogestioni.it	Ministry for the Economy and Finance Banca Italia Commission Nazionale per la Societa e la Borsa www.consob.it

	Trade body	Regulators
Luxembourg	ALFI Association Luxembourgeoise des Fonds d'Investissement www.alfi.lu	Government of the Grand Duchy of Luxembourg Institut Monetaire Luxembourgeois www.legilux.public.lu Commission de Surveillance du Secteur Financier (CSSF) www.cssf.lu
Spain	INVERCO Asociacion de Instituciones de Inversion Colectiva www.inverco.es	Comision Nacional del Mercado de Valores www.cnmv.es
UK	IMA Investment Management Association www.investmentuk.org	HM Treasury Financial Services Authority www.fsa.gov.uk
USA	ICI Investment Company Institute www.ici.org	Federal Reserve Board Securities and Exchange Commission www.sec.gov
Canada	IFIC The Investment Funds Institute of Canada www.ific.ca	Ministry of Finance The Canadian Securities Administrators www.csa-acvm.ca Provincial Securities Commissions Ontario www.osc.gov.on.ca Autorite des Marches Financiers, Quebec www.lautorite.qc.ca
South Africa	ACI Association of Collective Investments www.aut.org.za	Ministry of Finance Financial Service Board www.fsb.co.za

	Trade body	Regulators
Australia	IFSA Investment & Financial Services Association www.ifsa.com.au	The Federal Treasury Australian Prudential Regulation Authority www.apra.gov.au Australian Securities & Investments Commission www.asic.gov.au
China	SAC The Securities Association of China www.sac.net.cn	Ministry of Finance People's Bank of China China Securities and Regulatory Commission www.csrc.gov.cn
Hong Kong	HKIFA The Hong Kong Investment Funds Association www.hkifa.org.hk	Legislative Council of Government Securities and Futures Commission www.hksfc.org
India	AMFI Association of Mutual Funds in India www.amfiindia.com	Government of India Securities & Exchange Board of India www.sebi.gov.in
Japan	ITA The Investment Trusts Association, Japan www.toushin.or.jp	Cabinet Office/Ministry of Finance Financial Services Agency www.fsa.go.jp
Korea (Rep)	AMAK Asset Management Association of Korea www.amak.or.kr	Ministry of Finance and Economy Financial Supervisory Commission www.fsc.go.kr

INDEX

....

Index compiled by Terry Halliday